Please return on or before the date below.

Non-loan returns

Clifton Library
Rotherham College of Arts & Technology,
Eastwood Lane, Rotherham, S65 1EG
Need to renew or book a PC?
Call: (01709) 722869 or 722738

SOUND FOR THE STAGE

Patrick Finelli

ENTERTAINMENT
TECHNOLOGY PRESS

Application & Techniques
Series

SOUND FOR THE STAGE

Patrick Finelli

Entertainment Technology Press

Sound For The Stage

© Patrick Finelli
Revised drawings by Robert Eubanks

First published by Drama Book Publishers, New York, 1989.
This edition Published May 2002 by
Entertainment Technology Press Ltd
The Studio, High Green, Great Shelford, Cambridge, CB2 5EG
Internet: www.etnow.com

ISBN 1 904031 15 3

A title within the
Entertainment Technology Press Application & Techniques Series
Series editor: John Offord

CODE / SFTS002-11-02

CONTENTS

FOREWORD

At a time when our culture of digitally produced two-dimensional images seems to be nearing total saturation, when everything can be seen on TV and on the web and the impossible can be portrayed with astonishing detail on a movie screen, the complex sensory reality of live performance is, I would argue, more compelling now than ever before.

In no other entertainment medium do actors and audience breathe the same air, feel the same subway train rumble underneath or hear the same coughs from the back row. What's more: never does one audience hear the same thing the audience the night before heard. Sound - though vastly under appreciated as a theatrical design discipline - is uniquely positioned to inform, elucidate and even bend the temporal and physical reality in which theater thrives.

Over the last decade, I've had the privilege of working as a sound designer for several New York theater companies for whom sound design plays a primary creative role. For Richard Foreman's Ontological-Hysteric Theater, Target Margin Theater, my own company Elevator Repair Service, and especially for The Wooster Group, I've helped create productions in which sound functions not as decoration for scene changes, but as an active player in the action, changing night to night with the audience's reactions, the actors' performances and the weather. Whether it's Shakespeare's "Titus Andronicus" or Gertrude Stein's "Doctor Faustus Lights the Lights" I've found sound design to hold the greatest potential for exploiting theater's unique immediacy.

On my shelf sits a worn copy of this book, which I consider my only formal education in sound design. I clutched a copy of "Sound for the Stage" as I walked to my first interview with the Wooster Group ten years ago and although they didn't ask me the difference between a dynamic and a condenser microphone, it eased my nerves to know that I could tell them. Since then, this book has continued to serve as my primary sound design reference. It helped me start my career and I'm sure I'm not alone. I've no doubt its existence will continue to inspire others explore sound as a serious design element for a vital and important American theater.

John Collins,
New York City, 2002

INTRODUCTION

The audio aspect of theatre production has never been as complex or exciting as it is today. Virtually every production demands a microphone, music or sound cue. Directors, designers and technicians are confronted with numerous choices concerning reinforcement, recording, playback and special effects. Acoustic experts measure, test, tune and modify spaces to be acceptable to the trained listener's ear. The audio specialist has earned a place in the theatre as a key member of the collaborative artistic team.

On the stage, not only the physics, but the psychological properties of sound become important. The effect sound has in the theatre cannot be explained by mechanics alone. In addition to the physical cause, there is the physiological sensation which elicits a psychological response in the audience. The object is to move the audience, to create a world, suggest an environment, evoke an emotion, reveal truth. The ability of sound to reinforce a dramatic theme has been recognized by playwrights and directors for a long time. Communicating that idea to an audience accustomed to great fidelity at home and in the concert hall is a challenge for the sound designer, engineer and acoustician.

In every respect, the classical age represents the apotheosis of architectural and dramatic ideas. Every seat in the Greek and Roman theatre had a good view. The acoustics were perfect, so superb that the slightest sound on stage was heard by everyone. Epidaurus, the best preserved of the ancient theatres, built around 350 B.C., has extraordinary acoustic properties. This can be verified even today. A common match struck in the orchestra in front of the thymele will be heard perfectly from the highest vantage point among the 14,000 seats.

Another theatre of antiquity that has excellent acoustics is the Hellenistic theatre at Pergamum in Turkey. Built on a mountainside like a trembling reminder of another age, it is the steepest theatre in the world with seats at a 45-degree pitch. The Romans modified it in 160 B.C., adding sound towers at the top. Roman architects were noted for the effectiveness of their acoustics. Theatres and public buildings were all positioned for maximum sound efficiency. This theatre has a special advantage for high fidelity sound. Prevailing breezes that blow in from the sea each afternoon in theatre season not only provide an effective form of air-conditioning, but these winds carried with them the actors' voices up to the audience seated on the hillside. The Roman architect Vitruvius, writing in 15 B.C., mentions scene changes "when the gods enter to the accompaniment of sudden claps of thunder."

Sebastiano Serlio published *Architettura* in 1545 that dedicated one chapter to the Renaissance innovation of perspective settings. He acknowledges the need for sound effects in the English translation suggesting "Sometime you shall have occasion to shew thunder and lightning as the play requireth, then you must make thunder in this manner: commonly all Scenes are made at the end of a great Hall, whereas usually there is a Chamber above it, wherein you must roule a great Bullet of a Cannon or some other great Ordinance, and then counterfeit Thunder."

The *First Folio* of Shakespeare includes stage directions such as "alarums, excursions, flourish, trumpets and drums," especially in the history plays when the French and English armies engage in battle. The Prologue of *Henry V* contains a reference to the actual stage and the illusion that must be conveyed:

> *may we cram*
> *Within this wooden O the very casques*
> *That did affright the air of Agincourt.*
> *Think, when we talk of horses, that you see them*
> *Printing their proud hoofs i' the receiving earth.*

Gordon Craig, the great designer and prophet of the New Stagecraft, claimed that drama died when it went indoors. He expressed many complaints with prevailing theatre practice in his day and some of the problems may have been acoustic ones traceable to the evolution of the indoor performing space. In the sixteenth century, scholars looked to the Roman architect Vitruvius for models. Palladio designed the Teatro Olimpico in a semi-oval auditorium where staged academic readings took place in front of a richly decorated *scaenae frons* backed with doorways revealing the *papier maché* perspectives finished by Scamozzi. Aleotti created the first permanent proscenium arch in the U-shaped Teatro Farnese at Parma. The horseshoe-shaped auditorium with tiered seats and an orchestra pit was the norm from the baroque age until the nineteenth century. Since the middle of the seventeenth century when Italian opera burst upon Europe, theatres have been designed almost exclusively in a configuration best suited to operatic performances. Even Moliere performed in front of wing and border sets at the Palais-Royal.

Exactly what is meant by the modern theatre as perceived by Craig is:

> *The whole result as heard and seen on the stage: play, music,*
> *scene, acting, dancing, lighting, singing–all.*

Craig and Adolphe Appia are often mentioned together as torch-bearers of a new aesthetic. In his book *Music and the Stage Setting*, first published in

1899, Appia stresses the relationship between music and the plastic qualities of directional lighting. He reaches the conclusion that the arrangement of the stage is to be found in the rhythm of the music. Appia shows in detail, through analysis of the music-drama of Richard Wagner, that spatial forms are dictated by the nature and quality of the sound.

The importance of sound effects on stage and behind the scenes was realized by the Duke of Saxe-Meiningen, who revolutionized theatre production methods in the nineteenth century. The Meininger were noted for many innovations including the shrewd use of sound effects to heighten the emotional impact of the drama. Sound was used to reinforce the mood and elevate the activity of the imagination. His Berlin production of Schiller's *Fiesko* had a number of sounds: alarm bells heralding an assault, weapons pounding against iron-studded crossbars, axe-blows splintering heavy gates, explosions, bomb blasts, the clash of swords fading in the distance.

Stanislavski used a sound recording to solve a dramatic problem. In *My Life in Art*, he describes the staggering lesson he was given by a woman whom the Moscow Art Theatre brought back to Moscow in 1902 as a consultant on the milieu of *The Power of Darkness*:

> She interpreted the inner and outer contents of Tolstoy's tragedy so fully, truthfully, and in such bright colors, she justified each of our Naturalistic details of production to such an extent that she became irreplaceable to us. But when she left the stage and the regular actors of the company were on, their spiritual and physical imitation betrayed them...We made a final trial. We did not let her come on, but made her sing in the wings. But even this was dangerous for the actors. Then we made a phonograph record of her voice, and her song provided a background for the action without breaking up our ensemble.

Eugene O'Neill's *Emperor Jones* has a tom-tom accompaniment to the play. In the original production by the Provincetown Players this rhythmic device, which began at the beat of the normal heart, rose in tempo and volume until it filled the tiny Provincetown Playhouse with an ocean of sustained intensity and lifted the hearers out of their seats. Sound can have a powerful affective value in the theatre. It may even help to distract attention from flaws in a script.

Mordecai Gorelik, in his comprehensive treatise *New Theatres for Old*, provides several examples of dramatic sound effects in the plays of Eugene

O'Neill. In his 1922 play *The Hairy Ape*, the most powerful scene is that of the stokehole, with its noise, glaring furnaces, frightful heat and piercing whistles. The syncopated crunching of coal serves as an essential choral accompaniment.

Lee Simonson, in his book *The Stage is Set*, exhibits a memorandum sent by O'Neill to the Theatre Guild in 1929, shortly before his play *Dynamo* went into rehearsal. O'Neill comments on the importance of sound to his play. In this case the effects are thunder and lightning in Part One, and the sound of the water flowing over the near-by dam and the hum of the generator in Part Two:

> *I cannot stress too emphatically the importance of starting early in rehearsals to get these [sound] effects exactly right. It must be realized that these are not incidental noises but significant dramatic overtones that are an integral part of that composition in the theatre which is the whole play. If they are dismissed until the last dress rehearsals (the usual procedure in my experience), then the result must inevitably be an old melodrama thunderstorm, and a generator sounding obviously like a vacuum cleaner; not only will the true values of these effects be lost but they will make the play look foolish.*
>
> *I may seem to be a bug on the subject of sound in the theatre — but I have a reason. Someone once said that the difference between my plays and other contemporary work was that I always wrote primarily by ear for the ear, that most of my plays, even down to the rhythm of the dialogue, had the definite structural quality of a musical composition. The point here is that I have always used sound in plays as a structural part of them. This is a machine age which one would like to express as a background for lines in plays in overtones of characteristic, impelling and governing mechanical sound and rhythm–but how can one, unless a corresponding mechanical perfection in the theatre is a reliable string of the instrument (the theatre as a whole) on which one composes?*
>
> *Looking back on my plays in which significant mechanical sound and not music is called for (nearly all of the best ones) I can say that none of them has ever really been thoroughly done in the modern theatre although they were written for it. Some*

day I hope they will be—and people are due to be surprised by the added dramatic value—modern values—they will take on.
The great French theatre theorist and visionary madman Antonin Artaud thought of sound in another way, as a representation of an inner state, a magic sensation that infuses the spirit in subtle ways. Sound in Artaud's view is part of the language of theatre that "ensnares the organs" and "wildly tramples rhythms underfoot."

Artaud called for advanced research in sound. He wished to explore qualities and vibrations of absolutely new sounds which "present-day musical instruments do not possess and which require the revival of ancient and forgotten instruments or the invention of new ones." Artaud wanted sound to act in a visceral way, through the organs directly. He could be speaking about contemporary techno-industrial music when he suggests "research is also required, apart from music, into instruments and appliances which, based upon special combinations or new alloys of metal, can attain a new range and compass, producing sounds or noises that are unbearably piercing."

Artaud based important ideas on Balinese dancers he had seen in 1936. According to his impressions, "the sound itself is only the nostalgic representation of something else, a sort of magic state where sensations have become so subtle that they are a pleasure for the spirit to frequent." He expressed profound and radical ideas about sound. He treats the spectators like the snakecharmer's subjects, conducting them by means of their organisms to an apprehension of the subtlest notions, looking for sounds chosen more for their vibratory quality than for what they represent.

If you go to Broadway today, you can hear fantastic sound with over 100 wireless systems on everyone from backstage crew to lead singer. Flies, props, wardrobe and others operate on separate wireless systems. The musical *Rent* features wireless headset boom mics. Antennae are hidden under the floor and behind false prosceniums. Off-Broadway theatres may use MIDI and samplers so that one musician sounds like an entire orchestra. Digital technologies such as CAD, CD and Mini-disc are utilized for sound effects and atmosphere.

In 1996 I had the pleasure of seeing Al Pacino in Eugene O'Neill's *Hughie*. The sound design by John Gromada was excellent, especially the evocative atmospheric effects and microphone technique used for Paul Benedict's ethereal Night Clerk thoughts.

Unfortunately, this wonderful theatre piece was marred by an audible hum in the loudspeaker right in front of our seats. Undoubtedly, most of the audience would not have noticed the buzzing since everyone was enthralled by the riveting acting of a true star. However, I sat in the fourth row and heard it clearly despite an otherwise flawless production.

The persistent buzzing noise is often characteristic of electromagnetic and/or electrostatic interference. The troublesome frequency is often referred to as "60-cycle hum," but A/C power cables are only one possible cause of loudspeaker hum. Often the problem is inherent in the sound reinforcement and playback system, perhaps in the routing of speaker lines or the grounding of equipment.

Today, when some sort of sound is used in nearly every production from the lavish Broadway musical to regional out-door revivals, attention to this technical element is increasingly important. Accurate and appropriate sound reproduction is a requirement for every successful production. The new theatre artist must be able to create a dramatic idea with sound. Audience members are accustomed to exceptional audio clarity in the concert hall, the cinema and at home. Directors and designers agree that the audience should expect the same or better in the theatre. The sound designer must be capable of reinforcing the quietest whisper as well as the loudest crash in order to sustain the dramatic moment. While we look to the past for models, we must look to the present and future for the technology to realize those goals.

1 SOUND WAVES AND FREQUENCIES

Definition

Sound is the movement of air in the form of pressure waves that travel 1130 feet per second. A musical instrument creates a sound when its vibrations disturb the air molecules, creating a sound wave. Solids, liquids and gases will transmit sound waves, but a vacuum will not. Sound requires a medium of transmission.

Any vibratory motion of air particles will result in a sound wave. This provides one of the answers to a classic conundrum, if a tree falls in the forest, certainly the impact of the branches and trunk on other trees and the ground will vibrate surfaces sufficient to generate a sound wave. We could verify this if we placed a microphone and recorder at the site. The microphone section will help you learn how to test that hypothesis. Of course, this does not answer the many philosophical and phenomenological questions concerning the experience of sound. Our study involves both the physical generation of sound in space (acoustic) and the electrical analog called "signal," which may be recorded, created, stored and modified digitally.

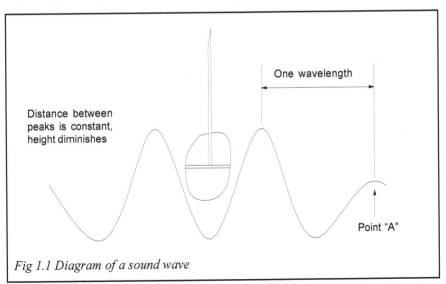

Fig 1.1 Diagram of a sound wave

Frequency

The back and forth motion of a piston creates a pressure wave. Refer to the figure above to see the analogous behavior of a rock on a string being dipped into a pool of water. The displacement and the rate of this reciprocating piston governs the curve of the pressure wave. Sound is created by a reciprocating motion of a piston in air. Frequency is defined as the number of times the pressure wave passes through a complete cycle in one second. In the case of the rock, the frequency of dips determines the wavelength. The size of the rock determines the initial amplitude of the waves. Point "A" shows that as the waves travel away from the source, they diminish in height (intensity), but the wavelength remains constant.

One cycle consists of the distance between peaks, a complete cycle being from peak to trough to peak. The number of cycles per second (CPS) determines the frequency of the sound. The amplitude of the waves determines loudness. In 1965, the term cycles per second was changed to Hertz (Hz) in honor of Heinrich Rudolf Hertz, an early German physicist. One cycle per second is stated as 1 Hz; 1 kilocycle as 1 kHz; 1 megacycle as 1 MHz. Either CPS or Hz may be used, but Hz is preferred. Human hearing extends from 20 to 20,000 Hz (20 kHz). A young, healthy ear is sensitive to the full range, but as a person gets older, sensitivity to the high end decreases. A normal adult may have an upper frequency limit of 14,000 Hz.

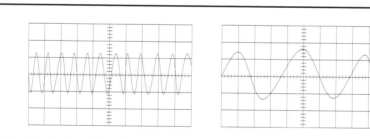

Fig 1.2 High and low frequency tones

Octaves

If a frequency is doubled or halved, that represents one octave. Frequencies between 16 and 32 Hz are called the first octave and are heard in the lowest tones of an organ. This range is also called the threshold of feeling. Frequencies between 32 and 512 Hz are considered the second through fifth octaves. The rhythmic low and upper bass frequencies are in this area. The sixth and seventh octaves are from 512 to 2048 Hz. If speech is limited to this frequency range, the sound will have a tinny, telephone quality. Over accentuation of these frequencies will cause listener fatigue. Emphasizing the eighth and ninth octaves, 2048 to 8192 Hz, adds presence to the sound. The human ear approaches its maximum sensitivity between 2000 and 4000 Hz. Lip and breath sounds are within this range and can be controlled through equalization.

The tenth octave consists of the region between 8192 and 16,000 Hz. These are responsible for brilliance in the sound. The tinkling of bells, triangle, cymbals and wind chimes are sounds that will benefit from emphasis of this octave.

White and Pink Noise

White noise is not an individual frequency but contains all sounds perceptible to the human ear. It is analogous to white light which contains all of the wavelengths in the light spectrum. The white noise waveform is sawtooth-shaped and consists of a fundamental frequency and even harmonics. It is not useful for calibration since the individual frequencies are not reproduced at equal energy levels.

Pink noise is similar to white noise, but, instead of a rising intensity, all frequencies are reproduced at an equal energy level. This makes measurement convenient. Pink noise is used by a Real Time Analyzer (RTA) for on-site audio spectrum analysis of sound reinforcement systems. The pink noise reproduced by the loudspeakers is detected by a microphone connected to the RTA. Individual frequency bands are displayed in real time, and the data may be used to determine an optimal equalization curve for the environment.

Pure tones can be generated by an oscillator built into a mixing board or tape player. A tone can be displayed on an oscilloscope as shown in figure 1.2. Notice the sine wave characteristic. The wave rises from zero to maximum in one direction, returns to zero in a symmetrical pattern, reverses direction and falls below zero to an equal magnitude, and returns to zero during one complete cycle.

Frequency Range - Musical Instruments

Sound is not always composed of a single frequency wave. It usually consists of many frequencies existing simultaneously. The list below gives a range of frequencies for musical instruments and other common sounds.

- Cymbals 340-12,000 Hz
- Snare Drum 70-15,000 Hz
- Tympani 40-5500 Hz
- Violin 180-8000 Hz
- Piano 60-8000 Hz
- Flute 250-9000 Hz
- Trumpet 160-10,000 Hz
- Trombone 70-7500 Hz
- Female Speech 170-10,000 Hz
- Male Speech 100-8500 Hz
- Hand Clapping 100-16,000 Hz
- Footsteps 70-15,000 Hz

Pitch

Pitch is the property of a musical tone determined by its frequency and intensity. The higher the frequency, the higher the pitch. Tuning to a pitch is also a matter of subjective taste. Today there is a controversy over the proper frequency to tune a violin. When Stradivari and other Cremonese masters were making their violins almost 300 years ago, everyone agreed that the pitch of A above middle C was around 420 CPS or 420 Hz. Since A is the tuning note on which other notes are based, first A is tuned in, then all strings are tightened accordingly. With A at 420, violins sounded warm and rich among the few other strings in a small chamber orchestra. As orchestras and concert halls got larger, musicians started to tune sharper, raising the pitch of A and therefore all other notes. During the life of Verdi, A was sharpened to 435 Hz at an international meeting in Vienna. In 1939, A was established at 440, corresponding to the 49th key on a standard 88-note piano. Currently, the demand is for even higher tunings of 443, 445, 450 and even 460 Hz.

Timbre

Timbre is used to describe the characteristic quality of a musical instrument which allows it to be differentiated from another. Timbre depends upon overtones, or harmonics. If all of the harmonics are removed by the use of filters, all instruments will sound the same, except for the pitch.

dB

A decibel, or dB is a logarithmic ratio of intensities. The sound levels encountered in daily life are numerous and vary over a large range of sound pressures. The dB measures SPL, or sound pressure level, which is normally calculated by expressing the sound pressure level with respect to a reference sound pressure, generally 0.0002 microbar for airborne sound. A more helpful relative indication of dB is charted below:

dB Environmental Equivalent

- 140 Jet aircraft at takeoff
- 130 Heavy metal concert
- 120 Noisy subway station
- 110 Machine shop
- 100 Large symphony orchestra
- 90 Cannery
- 80 Inside a moving car
- 70 Office meeting
- 60 Conversational speech
- 50 Average residence
- 40 Quiet neighborhood
- 30 Study in private home
- 20 Empty theatre
- 10 Inside a recording studio
- 0 Inside an anechoic chamber

Fletcher-Munson Observations

In the 1930s two researchers at the Bell Telephone Laboratories named Fletcher and Munson plotted a group of sensitivity curves for the human ear showing its characteristic for different intensity levels between the threshold of hearing and the threshold of feeling. The curves have been refined more recently by Robinson and Davidson. These data are often referred to as equal loudness contours. The reference frequency is 1000 Hz. Referring to Figure 1.3, it is clear that the contours are not equally spaced, but converge at the lower frequencies. This characteristic causes a change in the quality of reproduced sound when the volume level is changed. If it is desired to have two pure tones of equal loudness, for instance 1000 Hz and 50 Hz, and the 1000 Hz tone has an intensity level of plus 80 dB, following the curve out to 50 Hz indicates that an intensity level of plus 85 dB is required to make the 50 Hz tone sound as

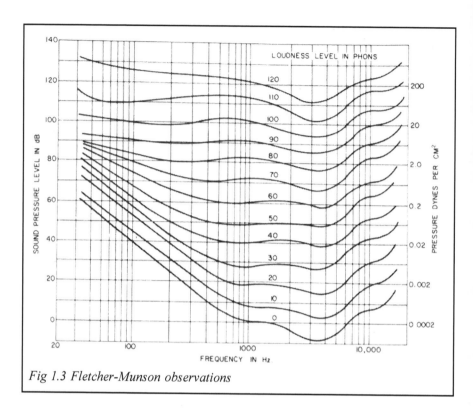

Fig 1.3 Fletcher-Munson observations

loud as the 1000 Hz tone, or a difference of 5 dB. If you lower the gain to where the 1000 Hz tone has an intensity level of plus 40 dB, following the curve out to 50 Hz, it can be seen that the intensity of this frequency must be increased to 72 dB to equal the loudness of the 1000 Hz tone, or an increase of 32 dB. Note that in lowering the level, the balance between the low and mid range frequencies has been destroyed, and to the ear it appears that the low frequency response is lacking. This is the principal reason for including a loudness control in home reproducing equipment. This also means that a monitor level in the studio must be established and maintained for consistency in recording.

Doppler Effect

An approaching ambulance siren appears to be higher pitched and louder than a receding siren. After passing the observer, the pitch and intensity drop quite rapidly until the sound fades completely. This is called the doppler effect. As the source approaches the listener, more cycles per second are being received than when it is going away. The increase in pitch is caused by compression of the sound wave as a result of the forward motion of the ambulance being added to the velocity of the sound wave. Conversely, as the ambulance moves away from the observer, the pitch decreases because the speed of recession is subtracted from the normal velocity of the sound wave, resulting in a lower pitch.

Reverberation

Reverberation occurs when sound is reflected several times between the surfaces of an enclosed space before reaching the ear. If it is greater than about 1.5 seconds, then direct speech tends to overlap and intelligibility is impaired. Both speech and music will be blurred and may become unintelligible because successive sounds overlap.

Phasing

The two components of phase are time and frequency. Different wavelengths will cancel each other out depending on the time of arrival and the frequency. It is possible to adjust the acoustic environment to reinforce a frequency. Similarly, it is also possible for frequencies to cancel each other out.

Standing waves occur when a sustained tone is emitted in an enclosure consisting of parallel walls. Anyone moving through the space will experience the sensation of an increase and decrease in the intensity of the sound, since the listener is passing through the zero and maximum points of the waves. Standing waves may be prevented by nonparallel walls, convex surfaces, multilevel ceiling sections and diffusers on the walls and ceilings.

A binaural head, which is a mannequin's head with microphones placed at the ear positions, may be used to determine the effects of phasing on the listener. The binaural head will only work for frequencies above 700 Hz, since lower wavelengths are so long that they seem to arrive simultaneously in phase.

In addition to the acoustic component, phase cancellation may also occur due to electrical problems in the hookup of loudspeakers or in the alignment of the drivers. See the loudspeaker section for more on that type of phasing.

Practicum

1. Play a test tape on a tape player and listen to pure tones at reference level.

2. Take a signal from the oscillator of a mixing board or tape recorder and route it through speakers with a constant gain. Then vary the frequency and observe what happens to sound perception. Notice how you must increase the intensity to hear low frequencies at the same level (Fletcher-Munson).

3. Play a tape or CD through a mixing console and adjust the tone controls to the extreme levels in order to hear the range of frequencies and how the music changes when you boost or cut the highs and lows. Begin to tune your ears to recognize frequency response characteristics at different points in the audio spectrum.

2 INPUTS AND OUTPUTS

Basic Electricity

There are two subatomic particles associated with electricity, but electricity is not atomic energy. The negatively charged electron moves about in the flow of electricity. The positively charged proton remains more or less fixed, providing the attraction that makes the electrons flow. Electricity is generated by detaching electrons from the atoms of materials by the application of energy, leaving the atoms in a state of unbalance; that is, there are more protons than electrons, and the result is a positive charge. Meanwhile, the extra energy which has detached the electrons causes them to accumulate at what is called the "negative" terminal. The difficulty comes in understanding that the electrons flow from a place of negative charge to a place of positive charge. In this sense the term "negative" denotes a surplus of electrons and the term "positive," a shortage.

Not all materials part easily with electrons from their atoms to produce a flow of electrons. Those materials that do allow electron flow are called conductors. Their electrons are detached easily and little energy is lost. Other materials part with electrons only with difficulty and with considerable loss of energy in the form of heat. These materials are known as poor conductors. Still other materials will release only a few electrons under any conditions. Such materials, called insulators, are used to isolate conductors from each other to keep electricity where we want it.

The basic pattern of any electrical circuit is: surplus of electrons, flow path, return to electron source. The elements of a circuit include:

1. a generator of electricity
2. a conductor to allow the electrons to flow
3. insulation to keep the electrons in the path
4. something to use the electrical energy
5. return conductor to allow electrons back to the generator

Impedance

Impedance is similar to resistance but the term impedance is reserved for use with alternating current (AC). For limiting the amount of current passing a given point, we can use resistors, inductors and capacitors. The unit of resistance used when measuring the resistance of resistors and the impedance of inductors and capacitors is called an ohm. Inductors and capacitors have another very important property in electronic circuits in that they have different effects on low and high frequencies. A simple tone control could consist of a selection of capacitors connected across the signal wires. Depending upon which capacitor is chosen, more or less of the high frequencies would be shorted out relative to the low frequencies.

Balanced and Unbalanced Lines

In addition to the voltage and impedance at inputs and outputs of equipment, we also need to know whether the connections are balanced or unbalanced. An unbalanced system uses interconnecting cables with one conductor and an overall braided screen, whereas a balanced system has two conductors plus a screen. It follows that plugs

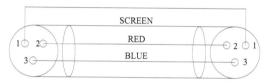

and receptacles for unbalanced systems need two pins or connections while for a balanced system three are required.

XLR, 1/4" Phone Plug, RCA and Other Connectors

The weakest link in any audio system is the interconnection between components. Expensive mixers, amplifiers and loudspeakers must be linked with cable and connectors. Faulty connections are responsible for a majority of sound problems. In order to ensure a solid connection, it is best to use a locking connector, such as a 3-pin XLR connector made by Switchcraft. These are used primarily for balanced lines and are often referred to as microphone or Cannon connectors. Neutrik also has a new XLR connector with automatic cable strain relief, solderless shield connection to pin 1 and/or shell, gold plated, polished tuning fork contacts and solder filled signal contacts (pin 2 and 3) for rapid soldering. An important feature is a secrure locking latch with a positive lock mechanism. The new versions of the XLR are specially designed for digital transmission. The shells can be coaxially linked to each other with a special locking ring. There are also special assembly tools available from the manufacturer that allow rapid and simple cable preparation.

Phone jack plugs are available in 2- and 3-pole configurations. It is a standard 1/4" plug and often used for connections between mixer and amp, or between mixer and effects or signal processing equipment.

Patch panels may have jack fields designed for the 1/4" phone plug. Patch panels are described in three different ways. A normalled patch bay maintains an internal signal connection between each panel input and output except when a plug is inserted, when the input or the output of the plugged cable takes over the signal path. A half-normalled patch bay maintains the internal signal connection even when a plug is inserted in the front panel output jack. This arrangement lets you maintain the internal connection while splitting the signal out the front panel output jack, which is very handy when you want send a signal somewhere else without losing your normal signal routing. A non-normalled patch bay has no internal signal connection; a patch cord must be used to carry the signal even when no external equipment needs to be inserted in the signal chain.

Some loudspeakers have a 1/4" jack, but it is recommended that a locking connector be used for theatrical loudspeakers. A two-pin twist lock connector is ideal for this purpose. Another alternative is the Neutrik locking connector. Many loudspeakers are fitted with Neutrik-brand Speakon® connectors which are noted for their ruggedness and secure contact. The Neutrik comes in two- and four-pole connector, so you could use it for bi-amping and bi-wiring. Many supply houses will make your cable to order with your choice of cable and connector. We suggest 14 AWG (refers to the diameter or gauge of the conductors, smaller AWG means larger current-carrying capacity) for the 4-pole and 12 AWG for the 2-pole conductors.

A loudspeaker or amplifier may have binding posts or banana jack receptacles. A problem with banana jacks is that they lose their spring after a while and must be "tweaked" to fit snugly. Again, it is recommended that the loudspeaker be converted to a locking connector. Neutrik makes a wide variety of XLR, 1/4" DIN and phono connectors, jacks, patch cables and accessories. One of their most outstanding products that is rapidly becoming an industry standard is the 2-

Fig 2.1 Rear Panel of the Allen & Heath GL 2200 Mixer

pole Speakon connector, an excellent choice for loudspeaker panels and cable connectors.

The RCA-type jack, also called a phono plug connector, is commonly found for line input and output on home audio equipment. It may be seen on the back plate of many cassette decks, CD players or integrated amplifiers. Molded plastic versions are available, but it is preferable to use the soldered metal plugs and jacks if you must use this type of connector.

Adapters are to be avoided as much as possible. Occasionally a converter may be needed with rented or borrowed equipment. But they are to be used with caution. An adapter may be matching two pieces of equipment without matching the impedance. Do not use an adapter to go from 3-pin XLR to 2-pin phone jack without using a line-matching transformer to go from low to high impedance or vice versa.

Wire and Cable

Always check your cable for continuity before running your microphone and headset lines. A cable tester (Appendix C) lets you check microphone, ¼" phone plug or phono cables by simply attaching both ends of the cable to the appropriate connectors and switching on a battery-powered circuit. Green LEDs signify that the cable works properly. Another feature is that the cable tester indicates the proper polarity. In the United States, pin 2 is always hot. In other countries this does not always hold true.

Microphone cables are vulnerable and must be handled with care. "Elbow wrapping" should be avoided since it forces tremendous twists and strains which may result in internal breakage. When wrapping cable, try to determine the natural way it wants to coil. Once in awhile, mic cable can be brought up to the grid in order to let it unwind and find its own shape. Then it is much easier to coil. Cable may be stored on pegs and color coded by length. When traveling with mic cables, use a case and store the cables without mic stands or any other equipment that may damage the cable. Remember, the most sophisticated equipment in the world will not work unless the cable and connectors have integrity (and continuity).

Multiconnectors and Snakes

Multicord cable is invaluable for sound reinforcement applications where a lot of microphones are used. Snakes can be made to your custom configuration by companies such as Wireworks. You may specify how many XLR or 1/4" phone plugs are on each end. You may have individual connectors on the mixer end of the snake and a box with receptacles on the stage end. Customized snakes are a key component in live stage applications

Fiber Optics

Optical fibers consist of a core material which carries the light, surrounded by a layer of cladding that reflects the light within the core. This reflection allows the signal to be transmitted through the optical fiber. Long-distance transmission systems use fibers with glass cores, referred to as "all-glass fibers." Fibers which use a glass core to carry light, but have a plastic or polymer cladding are called PCS (Polymer Clad Silica) fibers

Fiber optics offer several advantages over metallic systems. The transmitted signals are not distorted by any form of outside electronic, magnetic or radio frequency interference. Optical systems are immune to lightning or high voltage interference. They do not require grounding connections; the transmitter and receiver are electrically isolated and free from ground loop problems.

The simplest link consists of an optical transmitter and receiver connected by a length of optical cable. The optical transmitter converts the electronic signal voltage into optical power which is launched into the fiber by a light emitting diode (LED), laser diode (LD) or laser. The optical pulses are converted by a photodetector directly into a desired electrical signal. This process is closely analogous to the way old-fashioned crystal radios detected broadcast signals. A new approach, coherent communications, involves the use of two lasers, one at each end of the fiber optic link, plus the photodetector diode

Ground rules have been established to guide the technology in an orderly manner. One area in which a standard has been completed and the industry is producing components, is the Fiber Distributed Data Interface (FDDI). This is something like the computer standard interface RS-232, or the MIDI of fiber optics. FDDI is used extensively in computer networks. Transmission speeds for networks of 100 Mbps are standard in many large installations, with faster speeds and wider bandwidths on the horizon for the future.

Fiber optic cables are used for transmitting data between digital audio components. Sony's Minidisc comes with a converter box that takes the digital output of a CD player or DAT, which is usually transmitted via an RCA cable with conventional 1/4" phono plugs, and changes it into an optical digital input using special fiber optic cables and ports on the back of the component. You can connect two separate optical inputs this way and switch between them.

3 MIXING CONSOLES

Mixers

A mixing console or mixer is a device that allows you to take signals from several inputs, combine them in desired proportions and then route one or more of the signals to selected outputs at a level that can be handled by an amplifier. Although consoles come in all shapes and sizes, there are a few basic properties and characteristics that will help you no matter which mixer you select. A mixing console in the theatre may also be called a "sound board" in keeping with the way we refer to a lighting console as the "light board." The sound board operator controls the signal from an input by means of faders, buttons and knobs, and then routes the signal to recorders, special effects devices or power amplifiers.

Most mixers will accept both line and mic level signals. The sources may be music or dialogue from live microphones, CD or tape. Several separate audio signal sources may be combined into one composite signal or group of signals. Each mixer has a fixed number of input channels, output channels, assignment buttons or switches. Some mixers have equalization and allow you to select between line and mic inputs. Others may have only one type of input, requiring you to use an adapter and/or a line-matching transformer for an alternate input source. You may also find features such as phantom power, phase reversal, monitor options, auxiliary outputs and pre-fade listen capabilities.

Mixers are specified by the number of inputs and outputs. As an example, an 8 x 2 mixer will have eight inputs and two outputs, a 16 x 2 x 8 mixer will have sixteen inputs, two main outputs and eight submaster outputs. The versatility and complexity of the system increases with the number of input and output channels.

Each channel usually has its own preamplifier and tone controls. Mixers may be active or passive. Passive mixers use resistors and potentiometers, active mixers use amplifiers along with resistors to control gain or attenuation. The

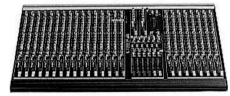

Fig 3.1 Allen & Heath GL2200 Mixing Console

Fig 3.2 Allen & Heath Xone:464 mixing

operator controls the relative levels of microphones, adjusts tone and selects the output destination. Auxiliary inputs and outputs may be used for special effects and monitor mixes. The stereo image of the sound is adjusted by balancing the amount of signal in each of the output channels. Movement of the sound may be accomplished in a similar way.

Most mixers amplify the signal from each microphone and add the amplified signals together to produce a single output that feeds a power amplifier and then loudspeakers. Each doubling of the number of microphones reduces the available gain before feedback by 3 dB. A large system may present a problem if the operator is not adept at operating faders and switching channels in and out of the system. Sometimes the feedback will expand more rapidly than the operator can respond. If the operator is not able to determine which microphone is causing the problem, the entire system must be shut down.

In the 1970s the concept of automatic microphone mixers was developed. A simple gate was inserted into each channel to shut the microphone down when it was not being used. These were called automatic mixers because the gain of the system was always adjusted to equal the gain with one open microphone. Newer automatic mixers use expansion instead of gating. This permits more versatile operation to hold mixer gain to the equivalent of one single microphone under constantly changing conditions.

The Input Channel

The figure above shows both input and output modules of the Allen & Heath Xone464 mixing console. The input channel can be operated in either microphone or line input modes. The input channel will have a MIC/LINE button, which provides a means of switching between mic and line inputs (1a).

The microphone input's low-level balanced impedance is usually greater than 2 k ohms, which will not cause any loading effects on normal microphones. The high level line input is unbalanced, with an input impedance of greater than 10k ohms.

The PAD button inserts a 20dB attenuator into the input of the microphone amplifier.

The MIC/LINE TRIM control is a detented potentiometer which can be used to vary the gain. In other words, it attenuates the amount of signal coming into the input channel.

Pressing the PHASE button will invert the phase on the input to correct for any mismatch.

Condenser microphones can be powered by an internal +48 volt power supply by pressing the PWR button (1e). Some mixing consoles made in England (e.g. Hill Audio) will have +32 volt phantom power, insufficient for some condenser microphones such as those made by Neumann. When using Direct Injection boxes, or unbalanced sources, the phantom power supply should not be switched on.

The input meter, often comprised of discrete LEDs, will indicate the input level as selected by the MIC/LINE switch.

The equalizer section allows areas of control over the audio spectrum. The high and the low frequency tone controls allow the board operator to boost or cut a range of frequencies. Often a mixer will have multiple levels of mid-range EQ controls which operate as parametric equalizers. The outer concentric knob lets you select a specific frequency within a specific range. The inner knob is then used to boost of cut the selected frequency.

The auxiliary section contains auxiliary send controls. Each control can be routed to selected auxiliary mix buses to give multiple sends for use as echo, foldback or other effects.

The routing section lets the channel input signal be routed to any or all of the group outputs and the stereo mix, by selecting the relevant routing button.

The Pan Pot is a center-detented control with slight signal loss at the center point. The Pan control may be placed in the signal path by pressing the PAN button. When the Pan control is not in the signal path any signal routed via the MIX button appears at equal level both left and right.

By selecting the MIX button, the signal is routed directly to the stereo mix bus.

The signal may be routed to any group by selecting the appropriate routing button. Mixers will often have the odd numbered outputs on the left side and even numbered on the right. Panning left will feed Groups 1 and 3, panning right will feed Groups 2 and 4.

The channel ON status is indicated by a green LED.

A red LED indicates the peak signal level at the insert send point, and illuminates at a level just below clipping.

The channel fader is a linear potentiometer.

PFL solos the pre-fader, post insert jack signal independently of the ON switch. PFL operation is indicated by a red LED on the channel and master warning LED on the Master Module.

The Output Channel

The Output channel is designed to control the final output for all of the inputs assigned to the module. If you have a 16x8x2 mixer, you have eight subgroup output bus modules for routing and two main output bus modules. A 16x4x2 will have four subgroup output bus modules. A signal derived at the input module can be independently sent to any or all of the subgoup outputs.

Pressing the ON switch switches the subgroup into operation.

The LED array meter monitors the output of the subgroup. The output is switched into operation by selecting the ON button.

The 3-band equalizer section with shelving type bass and treble and a fully parametric midfrequency section may be inserted into the effects return signal path, or used normally in the subgroup position. The shelving characteristic refers to the slope of the EQ curve. It does not keep rising with frequency, but, having reached the desired amount, flattens out, or "shelves," from that frequency on.

Effects send and returns assign the post-pan, post fader and effect return signals to the mix bus. The Pre/Post switch selects the effect return signal between pre and post effect control. The MUTE button mutes the signal.

The PAN control adjusts the relative balance of the subgroup signal into the left and right stereo without affecting the signal to the subgroup output.

The group output signal can be soloed with the AFL switch.

The group output channel fader is a linear potentiometer that controls the final output signal of the group.

The Direct Injection Box

In the age of electronic keyboards and other electrified musical instruments, a direct injection box is a mandatory piece of equipment. This device accepts an input signal that may be a high impedance or preamplified output. The direct box will then provide a balanced low impedance (150 ohms) signal for input to balanced low-Z equipment like a mixer or tape deck. The input is normally a 1/4" jack, as on the Whirlwind Director Direct Box. A loop-through 1/4" output is available as well as a male XLR jack for the balanced output. A switch which engages a -30 dB pad can be used for very hot instrument signals or for the speaker output of an amplifier. Another application is to route the output of a cinema projector through the DI box to the mixer and house sound system for improved fidelity. There is also a switch to insert a low-pass filter. The final feature, and one of the most important, is a ground lift switch which disconnects the ground between the input and balanced output.

Digital Mixing

There are two types of digital mixing: digital-controlled and all-digital. The digital-controlled system is one where the program material is still processed in its analog form, but faders, mutes, routing and equalization are controlled by a microprocessor. The all-digital system has an A/D converter at each input on the console and the signals are processed digitally. Professional all-digital consoles like the Neve DSP may cost upwards of $750,000. Professional digitally-controlled mixers like the SSL Series 4000 or other MIDI-based systems are available. An "affordable" digital mixer is the Yamaha DMP7, which is an 8 x 2 (8 inputs, 2 outputs) listing for less than $4000. It is a console with real-time MIDI-based automation of all functions and contains three programmable digital effects processors. The mixer processes streams of 16-bit numbers with 24-bit internal computation and a 44.1 kHz sampling rate. Changes can be recorded and recalled in internal memory locations, or in real-time via MIDI on a sequencer. It can be used for mixdown and live applications, especially since all parameters can be operated by external MIDI Note On/Off and controller commands. It also has motorized faders.

Surround Sound

Technology has a strong effect on the direction of sound reproduction. The strongest element in consumer and show sound is surround sound. Surround sound for feature films has been part of the industry for several years. Sound effects for films are increasingly sophisticated, home theatres are the norm. Basically, surround sound depends upon the delivery of separate sound efffects through a combination of front and rear stereo speakers, a center speaker and sometimes a low frequency "subwoofer." In order to accommodate this increasingly sophisticated taste for sound environments, spaces need to be redesigned, more speakers purchased and facilities rewired. The key to a surround sound installation is the mixing console. In the theatre, surround sound can be achieved by selected routing of program material through loudspeakers placed in strategic locations in the auditorium. For instance, in addition to the stage speakers, you may use loudspeakers designed to reproduce low frequencies behind or underneath the audience seating banks. Special sound effects might be delivered through speakers hung on the sides of the house. The source signals must then be routed via the mixer to the selected loudspeakers.

Practicum

1. Practice using the mixer in your theatre. Use microphone and line input sources, and experiment with equalization and routing functions.
2. Obtain a picture of the input or output module from the manual for your mixer and label the various switches and knobs.
3. Try to insert effects with auxiliary paths. Learn the practical difference between pre- and post send and return.

4 POWER AMPLIFIERS

Definition

An amplifier is an electrical circuit which transforms small voltages and currents into much larger ones with enough power to drive the cone of a loudspeaker.

At the heart of an amplifier is a device that controls flow-of-current on one terminal by a small voltage on an opposite terminal. This is analogous to a fast current of water controlled by a small force on the handle of a valve.

Vacuum tubes, transistors and magnetic fields are a few of the different devices used to accomplish this result. Some amplifiers can produce an output voltage (output) as much as 100 times the original voltage (input). A good amplifier is capable of changing a soft sound or low intensity signal (such as one transformed by a microphone and mixer) into a signal of much greater intensity than the original source.

Wattage and Rating

Amplifiers are rated using different factors for load and the results may mislead the user. If you see an amplifier advertised as providing 400 watts peak power, and another at 100 watts RMS, you may jump to the conclusion that the 400 watt amp has more power available. But you could be wrong. All manufacturers do not rate their amplifiers the same way.

It is possible to calculate the exact continuous average power from any amplifier. Just run a 1000 Hz signal into the amplifier input. Run the input up until the amplifier just starts to clip (distort). Now measure the AC voltage across the output load terminals. Take that voltage, square it, and divide that by the impedance (in ohms) of the output loss (the loudspeaker's im-

Fig 4.1 Crown K2 Series amplifiers

pedance in ohms). Suppose you measured 20 volts AC. Squared it would give you 400 watts, but only if there is an output loss of 1 ohm. However, very few amplifiers are loaded with 1-ohm loudspeakers. Most amplifiers are provided with terminals for 4 ohm, 8 ohm or 16 ohm loads.

RMS

RMS stands for Root Mean Squared. RMS power is calculated as:

$$RMS = (voltage)^2/load$$

For the amplifier in the previous example, here are the different results we can get with 20 volt, AC measured continuous power.

- 4 ohm load = 100 watts
- 8 ohm load = 50 watts
- 16 ohm load = 25 watts

It is easy to see how the power rating values can be manipulated. Many manufacturers will not tell the consumer what values were used to measure the RMS output. Always ask to see specification data before purchasing.

THD

Unwanted harmonics can be added to the original signal, adversely effecting the output of the amplifier. Total harmonic distortion (THD) is measured at rated power levels and usually ranges from about 0.1% to 0.25% of 20 to 20,000 Hz. Intermodulation distortion is measured for combinations of frequencies.

Connection to Mixer/Preamp

The amplifier is normally connected to a mixer or preamplifier by means of a line-level cable and connector. Although your home system may use RCA jacks, pro sound models use an XLR balanced connector. Balanced inputs are around 50k ohms and unbalanced are around 40 k ohms.

Output Impedance and Loading

The amplifier has terminals for attaching loudspeaker cables. Normally there are 4 ohm, 8 ohm and 16 ohm terminals. The amplifier must be loaded with the appropriate loudspeaker impedance. Remember to calculate the change in impedance with series or parallel hookups. For loudspeakers of the same impedance, in series the combined impedance is N (number of loudspeakers) times Y (impedance of one loudspeaker). In parallel, the combined impedance is Y divided by N. For example, two 8 ohm loudspeakers hooked in series have a combined impedance of N x Y = 16 ohms. In parallel, the same two loudspeakers have a combined impedance of Y / N = 4 ohms.

8-Ohm and 70-Volt Systems

An amplifier loaded with an 8-ohm loudspeaker is considered to be a low voltage system. Normally the manufacturer will state the correct working load for the amplifier. This may change depending on whether loudspeakers are switched on and off during a production, or if there are long runs of speaker cable, or if several loudspeakers are connected in series or series-parallel, which generally produces a high impedance load. In those cases a solution can be found by designing a high voltage system to feed the loudspeakers. This type of system is used primarily in auditorium paging applications, or running several speakers to dressing rooms, lobby, greenroom or box office. The loudspeakers are fed at high voltage (70 volts, for example) and transformers are placed to step down the 70 volts to 10 volts or below to feed the loudspeaker itself. For instance, a 40-watt amplifier can be used to feed two 10-watt capacity loudspeakers and four 5 watt loudspeakers with no loss of impedance. This high voltage system has the tremendous advantage of allowing loudspeakers to be switched on and off almost at random without affecting either the amplifier or the remaining loudspeakers.

Damping Factor

Amplifier damping has an effect on the performance of a loudspeaker. An amplifier with a high damping factor can control the motions of a loudspeaker cone better than an amplifier with a low damping factor. The damping factor of an amplifier is expressed as the ratio of loudspeaker impedance to amplifier source impedance. For a loudspeaker of 8-ohms impedance and an amplifier with an internal output impedance of 0.5 ohms, the damping factor is 16. It is important that the impedance seen by the loudspeaker "looking back into" the amplifier should be as low as possible because the loudspeaker cone is springy in its mounting. A large ratio improves the loudspeaker damping. A loudspeaker of 8-ohms impedance "looking back into" an amplifier of 0.16 ohms output impedance will have a damping factor of 50, a significant difference from the previous example. "Looking back into" is an expression used to designate the point from which a circuit is to be considered. The internal output impedance of the amplifier is the actual impedance seen when "looking into" the output terminals of the device. This internal impedance may be only a fraction of the specified load impedance. If a signal corresponding to a single push of the cone is fed to the amplifier, the cone moves forward, but when returning to its rest position it can overshoot and oscillate backwards and forwards for a few cycles. This extends the duration of the sound and is a kind of distortion. It must be kept to a minimum by damping the oscillations with as large a damping factor as possible. The Practicum at the end of this chapter gives an example of how speaker wire can affect the damping factor.

Transistors and Magnetic Fields

Most manufacturers build amplifiers with transistor or MOSFET (metal oxide silicon field effect transistor) technology. The original tube amplifier has given way to transistors, and then to MOSFETs, which are really just solid state tubes, but there have been few major breakthroughs in amplifier design before digital. The basic rule is that an amplifier that can provide super performance specs in the areas of slew rates, damping factor and distortion will be the one for professional operations.

Digital

The advent of digital technology has had a gradual but profound impact on power amplifier manufacturing. Manufacturers of power amps must consider that the digitalization of various audio components has increased performance expectations for their products. Digitalization has enabled pro audio users to decipher imperfections within an audio system, especially amplifier noise. As a result, manufacturers are seeking new ways to lower distortion rates, raise damping factors and eliminate magnetic hum.

Amps are the major link between microphone and speaker. They deal directly with high voltage. Digital technology is forcing every aspect of this process to become better. Previously, all an amp had to do was run a system. With the improvement in other components in the chain, such as signal processors and speakers, the importance of a high-quality amp has increased. Digital logic is used for remote control of settings, trouble shooting, and protection from short circuits and overheating. Problems can be tracked digitally rather than using mechanics to circumvent them. A lot of mechanical methods introduce distortion into the picture.

One path manufacturers are taking to incorporate digital technology into power amps is PWM (pulse width modulation), a switching technology used by class D amplifiers. PWM is employed by amplifiers that interpret sound according to the time lapse between signals of a constant voltage level, instead of relying on variations in the level of voltage.

Ninety-five percent of today's amps are linear, class B amps, which produce a lot of heat. Class A amps are primarily used in audiophile applications. They generate a substantial amount of heat and are too heavy and expensive for touring or most theatre applications. One problem with PWM amps is that radio interference from these amps tends to disrupt AM radio bands. Another is that the circuitry requires five times as many components. The more parts you have, the greater the possibility of failure. Another problem is the power supply. Current comes from the wall, and this poses a problem until clean digital power supplies can be developed.

Practicum

An amplifier has a damping factor of 50 for an 8 ohm load. What is the amplifier output impedance? To solve this problem, use the following formula:

Damping Factor = Normal Load Impedance/Amplifier Output Impedance
The amplifier output impedance is calculated thusly:
$50 = 8/x$
$x = 8/50$
$x = .16$ ohms (amp output impedance)

The amp is connected to a speaker by three meters of 22 gauge cable (ordinary two-color speaker cable). What is the total resistance of the cable if it has a resistance of 0.1 ohm/meter?
3 m x 0.1 ohm/m $= 0.3$ ohms

What is the damping factor if you consider the total impedance of amp plus cable?
Total impedance of amp plus cable: $0.3 + .16 = .46$
New damping factor: $D = 8/.46$
$D = 17.39$

The original damping factor was 50. Now, with ordinary cable, it has degraded to 17.39. What happens to the damping factor if we use 16 gauge lamp cord (zip cord) with a cable resistance of 0.024 ohm/meter? (assume same length)

New cable impedance: 0.024 x 3 = 0.072 ohms

Impedance of amp plus cable: 0.072 + .16 = .232

Recalculated damping factor: D=8 /.232

D= 34.48

The damping factor, the speaker cone's ability to oscillate efficiently, is significantly improved with a heavier gauge cable.

5 LOUDSPEAKERS

Most loudspeaker systems consist of one or more drivers installed in an enclosure. The picture below shows a dynamic cone driver. The driver consists of several parts, most prominent of which is the diaphragm, the shallow cone or rounded dome that is visible when the enclosure's grille is removed. Attached to the back of the cone or dome is a cylindrical bobbin on which is wound a coil of fine wire, the voice coil. The voice coil fits into a narrow circular slot in an assembly consisting of a

Fig 5.1 The JBL LSR32 Linear Spatial Reference Studio Monitor

permanent magnet and a surrounding structure of soft iron. The slot, or gap, has to be narrow in order to concentrate the magnet's field on the voice coil. A circular piece of spring-like corrugated fabric, called a spider, is used to guide the movement of the voice coil so that it remains centered in the narrow slot of the magnetic assembly. Woofers (low-frequency drivers), tweeters (high-frequency drivers), and mid-ranges are all made this way, though they differ in details. This description applies to dynamic loudspeakers, which represent the vast majority of speakers sold today. Electrostatic loudspeakers are constructed differently.

Dynamic Cone Loudspeakers

The combination of voice coil and magnetic assembly constitutes an electric motor designed to be driven by the output of an audio amplifier. The amplifier, in sending an audio signal to the speaker system, causes an electrical current to flow in the voice coil—a small current for small signals, a large one for loud musical passages. The flow of the current causes a varying magnetic field to be formed about the voice coil, and this

Fig 5.2 JBL 2235H Low Frequency Loudspeaker Component

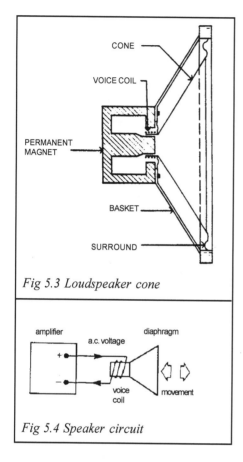

Fig 5.3 Loudspeaker cone

Fig 5.4 Speaker circuit

field, because of its interaction with the driver's magnet, causes the coil to move rapidly backward and forward (vibrate) in the magnetic assembly slot. And since the coil is attached directly to the diaphragm, it also moves, in turn imposing its vibratory motion on the air in the form of rapid pressure variations, otherwise known as sound.

The louder the sound a given speaker system is called upon to produce, the greater must be the current flowing through its voice coil and the longer the back-and-forth motions (excursions) performed by the voice coil/diaphragm assembly.

Aside from the obvious possibilities of direct physical abuse, like rupturing the diaphragm with a well-placed kick or dropping the whole loudspeaker down a flight of stairs, there are two common sources of loudspeaker damage: excessive voice coil excursion (especially in the woofer) and the buildup of excessive heat in the voice coil (especially in the tweeter).

For most music reproduced at average home loudness levels, the back-and-forth excursion of the voice coil is only a small fraction of an inch. This usually leaves enough excursion in reserve to handle the loudest musical moments on modern recordings, or even to permit a substantial increase in the volume-control setting. But if you ever drive the voice coil beyond its design range, several things can happen. The voice coil may be driven all the way back into the slot in the magnet structure so that it strikes the back plate of the assembly. This voice-coil bottoming is quite audible, often taking the form of a rapid clacking or clicking or even a hair-raising blatt. Another possibility is that excessive excursion will drive the voice coil so far forward that it pops out of its slot and fails to reenter it properly. This often results in permanent misalignment. The voice coil then rubs against the internal parts of the magnet assembly, causing a scraping or rattle on certain notes. Another possibility is that the coil could become jammed in the slot, preventing further movement altogether. Excessive excursion may also stretch or tear the fabric spider that holds the coil centered in the gap, or it may similarly damage the diaphragm where it is bonded to the metal frame of the driver. Finally, there are the wires that carry the electric current to the voice coil from the speaker's input terminals (or from the crossover). If the coil is vibrating back and forth too vigorously, these wires are flexed excessively and may fray and finally break.

When you play music loud, your amplifier puts more electrical current through the voice coils of your speakers. Whenever an electrical current flows in a wire some heating occurs, and the greater the current the hotter the wire becomes. That is why house wiring is equipped with fuses or circuit breakers to stop excessive current safely before it can overheat the wires in your walls and start a fire. There's not too much danger of fire inside your loudspeakers, but it is possible, by persistently playing music at excessive loudness levels, to build up enough voice-coil heat to melt the insulation of the voice-coil wires thus causing a short circuit, or to char the voice-coil form and the adhesive bonding the wire. Tweeters are particularly susceptible to this kind of damage, since their design requires low-mass voice coils with thin wire that heats up all the more quickly.

Compression Drivers

In a compression driven loudspeaker, the magnetic action is identical to, but the acoustic action is different from, a moving cone loudspeaker. The compression driver creates sound pressure waves directly. The thin metal diaphragm of a compression driver acts to compress a volume of air in the pressure chamber. The chamber is vented to the outside by a narrow throat leading into a horn-type radiator. The horn couples the varying pressures in the throat to the air of the room. The compression driver is able to overcome many of the high-frequency break-up problems of the cone driver. Modern compression drivers are able to operate to the upper limits of hearing at very high levels with low distortion.

Fig 5.5 JBL 2370A Bi-radial Horn

Subject to the same mechanical and thermal

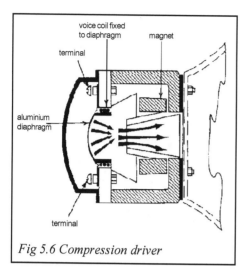

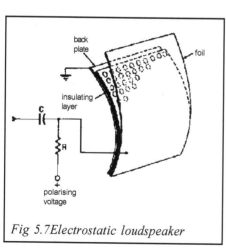

limitations as the cone driver, the compression driver is a more delicate device and will withstand less overload abuse than the typical cone unit. Two great killers of compression drivers are mechanical failure due to excessive power at the low end of its operating range and thermal burnout due to feedback. Compression drivers dislike feedback and low frequencies.

Two major speaker manufacturers, EV and JBL, have designed compression drivers

Fig 5.6 Compression driver

containing neodymium, a highly magnetic material which allows for a decrease in size and weight of the driver and a 1 dB increase in efficiency over comparable ferrite models. Compression drivers are never used in the bass region. While a few operate as low as 300 Hz, most are rated for use above 500 Hz, and some operate only as super tweeters above 5 kHz.

Electrostatic Loudspeakers

The electrostatic loudspeaker is made up of a heavy metal plate and a very thin, lightweight metal foil separated by an insulating layer. The plates are charged with a very high voltage–positive on one and negative on the other –thus creating an electrostatic potential between the plates. An audio voltage is superimposed on one of the polarizing voltages causing the potential between the plates to vary in step with the audio. As the electrostatic force changes, the thin foil plate will vibrate in step with the changing audio signal. This movement is passed on to the air

Fig 5.7Electrostatic loudspeaker

around the plate, thus creating sound waves. Electrostatic loudspeakers can do an outstanding job of reproducing the higher sound frequencies, from about 1000 Hz up. They are quite unsatisfactory in bass reproduction since the foil plate cannot make the large movements required to create long wavelengths with useful intensities. These loudspeakers are used as high-frequency units in some very good and expensive home systems. But they are of no use in theatres because they do not have capacity for high volume.

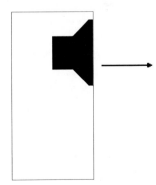

Enclosures

A loudspeaker is an electromechanical device for converting a varying audio voltage into corresponding sound waves. In loudspeaker design, the goals are to limit distortion and to reproduce accurately the audio frequency response of the amplifier. Should it always be flat? Not necessarily. Some loudspeakers have been designed to respond more favorably to certain frequencies than others, such as bass reflex speakers. Loudspeaker enclosures are measured by their resonant frequency, or Q. This refers to the frequencies that the box reproduces best.

Fig 5.8 Loudspeaker enclosure

Damping of the loudspeaker enclosure is the process of reducing unwanted resonant effects by applying absorbent materials to the surfaces. Successful damping expresses the ability of the cone to stop moving as soon as the electrical input signal ceases. Poor damping allows motion to continue briefly, like an automobile with poor shock absorbers. This hangover creates a booming sound in the bass frequencies masking clarity.

The Closed Box

The closed box cabinet may be described as an infinite baffle, because the waves emerging from the back of the cone cannot reach the front of the loudspeaker–they have an infinite path length. These cabinets have a poor low-frequency response.

Fig 5.9 'Closed box' speaker enclosure

Fig 5.10 JBL Array
Series 4892
Loudspeaker

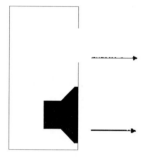

Fig 5.11 Bass reflex
enclosure

The Vented Box / Bass Reflex

The simplest and best low-bass enclosure is the vented box. The old name for this enclosure is bass reflex. A box of the proper volume is tuned by adjusting the area of the vent to match the needs of the driver. Sometimes it is also necessary to add a duct behind the vent to tune the system. By proper selection of box volume and duct/vent size, a given driver may be operated smoothly to very low bass – say 30 Hz – or it may be made to roll off smoothly at some higher frequency as, for example, in a stage monitor where low bass might cause feedback problems.

Although this concept has been around as long as loudspeakers, there was no reliable mathematical formula for calculating box, vent and duct sizes. It was a matter of experimenting in the workshop until a good combination was found. Failures were so common that most manufacturers for the home market stuck with the closed box which was much easier to get right. Manufacturers of high-power professional equipment used the horn. But Dr. Small and Dr. Thiele from Australia, in a series of articles printed in 1961, and reprinted ten years later in the United States, provided simple-to-use and very reliable formulas to design vented boxes. The vented box is as much as 10 times more efficient (louder) than the sealed box and has a better low-end response. The vented box is not quite as efficient as the horn, but it has a much better low-bass response at a very much smaller size, weight, and cost.

The directional pattern of a cone driver in a vented box is very predictable based upon the dimensions of the box and size of the cone. All bass enclosures are completely nondirectional at low frequencies. Remember that at 50 Hz, the wavelength is 22 feet. It just wraps right around a small box like it wasn't even there. Around 100 to 200 Hz, depending on box size, the directivity begins to narrow down to 160 degrees and holds there up to the frequency whose wavelength is the same as the cone diameter (piston range). At that point, the beam begins to narrow at the rate of 50% per octave.

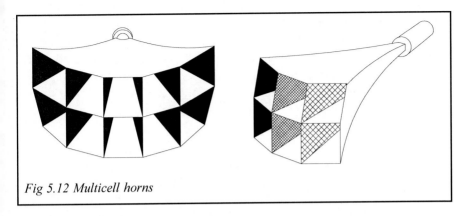

Fig 5.12 Multicell horns

Multicell Horns

There are about a half dozen types of high-frequency horns that may be used with a compression driver. The radial horn came first and is the most widely used of all horns. Its biggest problem is that it does not disperse all frequencies equally. As the frequency rises the coverage angle grows progressively narrower. This is called beaming. In an effort to reduce the beaming problem, the multicell horn was created. The multicell is just a group of small horns connected to a common throat. This scheme does not eliminate beaming, it just changes it.

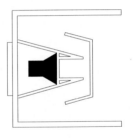

Fig 5.13 Folded horn

Folded Horns

Some horns are being built to operate lower than 150 Hz, but the size gets very large. Remember that mouth size and length determine the low-frequency limits. One way of increasing low-frequency response while maintaining reasonable horn size is to fold the horn. This scheme works well at low frequencies but cannot be used above a few hundred Hertz because the shorter wavelengths begin to distort as they move around the corners.

An excellent example of the folded horn loudspeaker is provided by Klipsch, one of the leading manufacturers of this type of loudspeaker (fig 5.14).

Fig 5.14 The Klipsch La Scala folded horn

Resonant Frequency

Drivers are designed and built to reproduce a specific range of frequencies. Thus, there are low, mid and high frequency drivers. The resonant frequency of a driver is determined by hanging the speaker in free air, away from reflecting surfaces. An oscillator is run through a power amp to drive the speaker from 20 to 20,000 Hz. At the resonant frequency, the excursion of the diaphragm will be at its maximum.

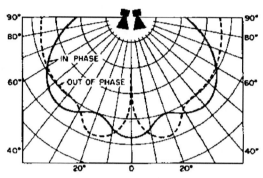

Fig 5.15 Speaker phasing

Phasing

In loudspeaker systems that use two or more units, it is essential that the diaphragm of each loudspeaker be in acoustic phase with each other. The diaphragms must all move in the same direction at a given instant. When a system is out of phase, it will have a good low-frequency response as well as a good high-frequency response, but the overall response will be lacking in presence. The phasing can be checked electrically by making sure that the plus and minus terminals of the speaker are wired the same way.

A signal of the same frequency as that of the crossover point can be applied to the input of the system. As the oscillator is moved over a small band of frequencies above and below the crossover frequency, the listener should hear a smooth crossover. If the units are out of phase, a null point will be noted.

It is also possible that alignment of drivers could be the reason for phase cancellation. If the system consists of a multicell horn and low-frequency driver it can be

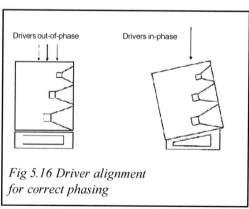

Fig 5.16 Driver alignment for correct phasing

improved by moving the horn forward and back until a position is found where a considerable improvement is heard in the quality of reproduction. A stand can be constructed to slant the speaker back, bringing the drivers closer to the proper alignment.

Acoustic Coupling

Dr. Amar Bose, professor of electrical engineering at MIT, recognized that it isn't just a speaker's frequency response that determines its sound. He knew that it had something to do with the way sound was projected into the listening room. Theoretical acoustics say that the ideal sound source is a single point radiating

Fig 5.17 Bose 901®Series VI Direct/Reflecting® speaker system

sound energy in all directions. Dr. Bose proceeded to design the Bose 901 loudspeaker which utilizes acoustic coupling and direct reflection. The Bose 901s have a unique design which consists of nine identical drivers connected in series. The impedance of each driver is 0.9 ohm. The total impedance is 8.1 ohms. Acoustic coupling refers to the phenomenon that drivers connected in series cannot resonate at the same frequency, so the cones divide the frequencies and reproduce accordingly. Sound projection is from the front and back, eight drivers reflecting off the corner wall surface and one in the front to help imaging and stereo location. The effect is that the listener feels immersed in the music.

Crossovers

A crossover is a circuit that divides the signal from an amplifier into frequency bands to feed appropriate loudspeakers, i.e. high frequencies to the tweeter and low frequencies to the woofer. Passive crossovers are merely capacitance circuits;

Fig 5.18 Bose 802 Platinum System Components

active crossovers are electronic, which may allow frequency and range parameters to be defined or changed.

Hints on Using Loudspeakers

1. Never hook up a speaker when the amplifier is on and being driven by a signal.
2. Avoid feedback: high-frequency compression drivers can very quickly be overpowered by sustained feedback.
3. Always us a DC blocking capacitor on high-frequency compression drivers when bi-amping to protect them from turn-on transients and spurious low-frequency signals.
4. Never turn on low level electronics (mixer, graphic equalizer, etc.) after the power amplifiers are on.
5. Keep dust, dirt, Coca-Cola, beer, popcorn, etc., out of the throat of the high-frequency horn. They present an increased load on the driver and significantly reduce high-frequency output.
6. Avoid ground loops: ground loops and high power amplifiers may be fatal to loudspeakers. Do not make connections to equipment with levels up or power amps on. Use connectors that make ground connections first. Keep cables in good repair. Please refer to the **Wire and Connectors** section for more information on loudspeaker connectors.
7. Avoid excessive low-frequency signals as severe cone damage can result. Use high pass filters—40-60 Hz, 10 dB/octave.
8. Do not run power amplifiers into clipping as this will reduce both amplifier and speaker life expectancy.
9. A strong grille should be used on floor monitors to prevent foreign objects from piercing the cone. A metal or plastic screen should be used in taverns and cabarets.
10. Casters may help, but when moving heavy speaker cabinets and amp racks, secure them to avoid runaways.
11. A solid support for the speaker system is a necessity. Poorly braced platforms can collapse.
12. Always use a power amplifier with protection against DC voltage at the outputs. Dead output transistors can put the voltage through the voice coil. The power supply current can blow out the voice coil before the fuse has a chance to react.

13. Make a habit of checking the mounting bolts or clamps on speakers for tightness regularly.
14. Avoid excessive equalization. Also, avoid frequency extremes when equalizing as they present demands that most speakers and amplifiers can't handle, especially in live sound reinforcement.
15. Store speakers in areas that maintain fairly even temperature and humidity and not extremes of either.
16. When using a speaker system outdoors keep weather protection handy. Even a small amount of rain or water can damage the bass speaker cone and cause rusting of the internal surface of the drivers.
17. When transporting multicell or fiberglass horns put them into travel cases. It is also advisable to use a hard cover over speakers when transporting them.
18. Always use proper grounding.
19. Use a logical approach when stacking a speaker system and provide a stable structure even at the expense of coverage area.

Practicum

1. Hookup several different types of loudspeakers next to each other and play the same sound through them one at a time. Compare the frequency response by listening to how the speaker reproduces highs, mids and lows. You will be able to judge which of your speakers adds warmth, color and brightness, and which act as low-pass filters. Future decisions on loudspeaker selection and placement will benefit from this type of analysis.

2. Take a damaged loudspeaker, or an old one that is not used anymore, and take it apart. Carefully analyze the driver. Describe and list the parts of the cone assembly including voice coil, magnet, spider and diaphragm.

6 MICROPHONES

A microphone is one of the most important sources of sound in the theatre. Whether you are amplifying the voice of a singer or actor, reinforcing a musical instrument or recording a

Fig 6.1 Shure SM-58

performance, the selection and placement of microphones can make or break your production. A microphone is basically a transducer, which is a device that converts acoustic energy (voice or other sound) into electrical signals. We input the signals into the mixer where we can modulate, control and combine with other signals before routing the output to amplifiers and loudspeakers. We can categorize microphones according to their physical characteristics, directionality, transducer type and impedance. Most of the microphones used in professional audio applications are low impedance. There are two basic transducer types of microphones used in the theatre, dynamic and condenser, that come in a variety of shapes and sizes.

Dynamic Microphones

A dynamic microphone has a diaphragm that moves a coil inside a magnetic field to generate an electrical signal. It requires no phantom power and is the most rugged of all.

Moving coil. The most common professional type of dynamic microphone is the moving coil. It operates on the principle that an electrical voltage will be generated in a conductor moving inside a strong magnetic field. Sound pressure waves cause the diaphragm to move. The motion of the diaphragm is passed on to a coil of very fine wire that is centered around a rod of a strong magnet. The first moving coil was introduced by Western Electric in the late 1920s.

Moving ribbon microphone. The moving ribbon operates on the same principle as the moving coil except that here the diaphragm and coil are combined into a single element. They are noted for warm sound and good bass response. A weakness is that they are very fragile. They are great for recording voice (radio narration). After World War II, the RCA 77A ribbon dominated the market in the United States. It was smaller and more portable than a comparable condenser microphone. In 1952, General Eisenhower was entering the race for the presidency. He asked his friend General Sarnoff of RCA for a high-quality microphone that would be small enough not to hide his face. This was the genesis of the RCA Bk-5, the first small ribbon microphone, measuring about one inch in diameter and about six inches in length.

Microphone response curves. Microphones have characteristic response curves and are sensitive to particular ranges of sound. For example, the SM-58 rolls off at 100 Hz and 8,000 Hz. It has a big 6 dB peak around 3,000 Hz to 5,000 Hz. This makes it a dynamite mic for vocals. Figure 15 shows a picture of the most popular vocal microphone in the world.

Condenser Microphones

The first high-quality professional microphone developed was a condenser. It was used in the 1910s as an instrumentation microphone. Its frequency response range is normally from below to above the audible range. It consists of a pair of plates, one or both of which can be diaphragms. The two plates are charged with an electrical potential. When the sound pressure waves cause the diaphragm plate to vibrate, the vibration alters the distance, hence the capacitance, between the two plates, thus allowing a very small electrical current to flow. This feeble current from the condenser plates must be amplified right at the condenser. It is crucial that no more than a few inches separate the plates from the amplifier.

Since the diaphragm is a condenser element, it requires power and electronics. Some types use a battery mounted in the microphone housing. Now it is no problem to build a tiny amplifier no more than an inch in diameter into the case of the microphone. But when they were first used in 1920s and 1930s, the power supply was a large heavy box with the microphone element in one end.

The condenser microphone is more fragile than the dynamic and works well for brass and strings. On-axis response changes in the mid-bass region depending on how close the sound source is to the mic. The difference in bass sounds can be enormous.

Fig 6.2 Shure SM87A Supercardioid Condenser Microphone

Super-cardioid. The super-cardioid is manufactured by adding tubes and more rear holes to the chamber. This makes a tighter cardioid pattern with greater back rejection, a reduction in off-axis coloration and a reduction in the proximity effect (see page 64). Most of the hypercardioid microphones are shotguns with severe off-axis coloration and are often best used only for speech pick-up.

Acoustic cardioid. There is an easy way to make a cardioid with only one element instead of two. It was discovered by accident. At RCA labs a polar response of an omnidirectional mic was found to have a cardioid pattern. The technician had done a poor job of soldering. He had left a small hole in the rear pressure chamber and accidentally created the first acoustical (rather than electrical) cardioid microphone.

PZM - Pressure Zone Microphones

A pressure zone microphone consists of a small metal plate upon which is mounted a small block with an XLR connector in one end. The microphone element (a condenser) is less than 1/4" in diameter and is mounted facing the metal plate with only a few thousandths of an inch space between them. There is no such thing as on-axis; all the sounds reaching the PZM will come in along the mounting plate in what is known as the boundary pressure zone.

The PZM is rarely mounted on a mic stand: it goes on the floor, on the ceiling, on a set wall, or attached to the piano lid. Its pickup pattern is hemispherical–one half of an omni. It has no off-axis coloration. A pressure-calibrated electret capsule is mounted parallel to an acoustic boundary and within a very short distance of the boundary. This allows the transducer to operate within the pressure zone formed by the combination of the incident and reflected waves of the boundary. Incident and reflected waves are in phase and do not produce comb filters which are reinforcement and cancellation effects in the response due to phase differences which develop further away from the boundary. By operating in the pressure zone, the PZM does not encounter the comb filters produced by that boundary, and thus can have a smoother response than a free-field mi-crophone, which in most cases will be operated several feet from the nearest boundary. The pressure zone also serves to integrate the direct and random incidence sound fields at the bound-ary so that the PZM responds to both equally.

Fig 6.3 Crown PZM 30-D

Fig 6.4 Crown
PCC 160

Free-field microphones display different response curves to the direct and random incidence fields in which they operate, which often produce a result that does not sound natural. PZMs have smooth sounding response and transparent natural sound.

An additional benefit is that the annoying noise characteristic of microphones when accidently rubbed or touched is practically eliminated with the various PZM and tie-bar models. This is due to their small diaphragm mass and the special mounting material which provides isolation between the capsule and the microphone body.

The PCC 160 by Crown is similar to a PZM, but it has a half supercardioid pattern. Current practice has found the phase-coherent electret condenser PCC 160 to be superior to the PZM for floor microphone applications in a musical or review. Three of them can cover an entire 50' proscenium opening. It is an electret condenser supercardioid microphone that will work lecterns and conference tables.

Wireless

We often use wireless microphones in the theatre which presents another set of requirements in terms of placement of the transducer element, transmitters, antennae and receivers. Large musicals such as *Showboat* and *Rent* may use twenty or more wireless mics. Wireless technology frees the actor/singer from the encumbrance of cables and stands.

Wireless microphones of many types are available to reinforce a performer's voice. A hand-held wireless microphone can be used when the actor or singer wants to move without a cord. Lately we have seen frequent use of

Fig 6.5 Nady UHF 760
Wireless System

headset "boom" microphone mounts, first popularized in the rock n' roll industry, clearly visible to the audience. This interferes greatly with enjoyment of period drama. Rather than attempt to hide the wireless mic, some shows can get away with placing the condenser element in the best location possible relative to the actor's mouth. Broadway shows such as *Rent* do not conceal the fact that wireless mics are used, although the antennae are hidden under the wooden stage floor of the Nederlander Theatre. You should work with your costume designer and wardrobe staff to design pouches to place the transmitter. It can range from an inside pocket of a coat or a holster in a harness worn under clothing or even a pouch on a thigh-mount garter.

Although there are many hand-held wireless mics in use and boom mics are rearing their ugly heads on the stage, more often we use lavalier mics in the theatre such as the Sennheiser MK-2. If the object is not to see the microphone, a lavalier connected to a transmitter is the answer. It is important to place the microphone element in close proximity to the performer's mouth. Using a lapel clip or an alligator clip for a lavalier microphone is not always the best solution, since the actor may turn her head from side to side away from the microphone's optimal sensitivity pattern. There are several ways of placing a wireless microphone element on an actor. Jim van Bergen is an award-winning sound designer (*Art, True West*) who has developed many innovative techniques for wireless microphone placement including magnet, earloop, transpore, tegaderm, and elasticized thread. A magnet on a pendant or in a pocket may be used to attach the mic element through clothing. Earloops can be almost invisible if you use a flesh-colored gasket to cover the wire and transpore adhesive tape for attaching the mic element. Tegaderm (transparent, useful for dancers), blenderm (for allergic performers) or topstick (a hairpiece tape) are other adhesives for attaching a mic element to an earloop or to the skin. Elastic thread might be the best solution if an actor has hair or a wig since it can be blended with the hair and you'll be able to place the mic right over the actor's forehead. Remember to use a small piece of tape on the back of the actor's neck to guide the wire to the transmitter.

Often we will place the microphone in the actor's hair, or in *Phantom of the Opera*, right under the mask, routing the cable to the transmitter placed in the small of the back. This may occasionally present a problem, as in the University of South Florida's production of *The Tempest*, where a nearly-naked Ariel had to have a wireless microphone for a pitch-changed voice. Ultimately, it was taped within his loin cloth. When you have to mount a wireless transmitter on an actor's body, the unit must be protected against substances that may interfere with the electronics. Wrap the transmitter in a non-lubricated prophylactic and insert cotton at the top to absorb perspiration before attaching it to the body with surgical tape and then adhesive. Small plastic bags may also be used for this purpose. The foam surgical tape will protect the performer's skin, then you can apply the adhesive on top. Be forewarned that you may receive strange reactions from the cashier at your local drugstore when you purchase batteries, condoms and surgical tape for your wireless system.

Recent decisions by the FCC might congest the UHF television spectrum which will affect UHF wireless microphone systems. VHF Synthesized Wireless Microphone Systems supersede the conventional wireless concept. The PLL (Phase Locked Loop) synthesized tuning makes it simple to switch operating frequencies for interference-free operation anywhere. The Sony diversity system uses two transmitter antennae placed apart from each other to simultaneously receive signals of a single wireless microphone or transmitter. The tuner provides two switching control voltages in proportion to the field strength of the incoming signals at each antenna, and comparing these voltages, the tuner automatically selects the stronger input from moment to moment, and delivers it as the output, thus maintaining stable reception with an excellent signal-to-noise ratio. This eliminates antenna dropout and reflection phase cancellation.

The Sony wireless microphone has a built-in limiter and compressor and a frequency range of 30 to 18,000 Hz. The transmitter operates on the 200 MHz VHF band (174.6 MHz to 215.4 MHz) which corresponds to TV channels 7 through 13 in the United States. Channels are allocated in a clever way. Each of the 7 available TV channels is divided into 24 wireless microphone channels with separation of 200 kHz, giving a total of 168 potentially usable channels. The diversity tuner allows pushbutton selection of any of these channels. A signal having wide dynamic range is compressed for transmission on a narrow-band channel and then expanded by the tuner to restore the original signal. Please note that the use of wireless devices is regulated by the Federal Communications Commission and requires an appropriate license.

The newest technology in wireless systems is UHF band. You get better performance in terms of audio quality and better RF performance because the antennas are more efficient. Some users upgrade from VHF. Multifrequency systems have made wireless more complex and in some cases overwhelming. Current Broadway shows are exploiting wireless technology to the maximum. *Showboat* uses approximately 100 wireless systems - 48 used by performers, plus wireless intercoms, personal monitor systems and others. You need excellent filtering, shielding and headroom. You need to prevent interference among the channels, a clean signal if you tune to 700, you want to have 700 and not 690 or 680 MHz.

There is a wide range of pricing for wireless systems. You can purchase a basic hand-held transmitter and receiver for less than $200 or spend upwards of $10,000 per channel.

Caution: The dimming of lights may produce electrical interference over the entire frequency of range of 1 MHz to about 100 MHz. Position the antenna and the wireless microphone or transmitter in a place where such interference is at a minimum.

C-Tape

C-Tape is commonly called a contact microphone. The transducer is a flexible strip of plastic approximately 3 inches wide and either 3 or 8 inches in length. It is sandwiched between two outer layers of plastic. C-Tape is fully flexible and capable of being wound around a pencil. Basically, it is a co-axial transducer with the central element being a flat foil. Around this is wrapped an earthing element. There is a change in capacitance between the inner foil and the outer earthing layer, and the inner foil itself is covered in C-tape's own piezo-electric vinyl–a material like an electret or plastic with a lot of free electron activity in the outer layers. The transducer uses these two effects, the pressure sensitivity on the inner foil and the change in capacitance to convert the sound pressure into electrical signals.

The transducer has the following characteristics:

1. It has a mode of operation that is essentially capacitive but with an electret enhancement.
2. It is a thin tape, 13mm wide, which covers a finite area of the instrument soundboard.
3. It has a density low enough not to significantly damp the vibration surface.
4. It is totally flexible and will thus conform to the curved body of a violin, double bass or drum shell.

C-Tape was originally designed for use on the drum, where experiment has shown that the closest sound is achieved by its attachment to the inside of the shell.

Phasing

When you speak into a mic, the diaphragm pushes forward and causes a voltage to appear at the connector. The voltage can be either positive or negative, depending on how the connector is wired. If the wires are reversed on pins #2 and 3, and two mics are brought together, the sound will cancel. Take one mic, mark it as a reference, and compare all the rest of the mics to it.

It is best to keep microphones 3 to 4 feet apart when the user is within a 1' distance of a microphone.

When placing microphones for a vocalist, instrument or other equipment, place your ear where the microphone is to hear what it is hearing.

Proximity Effect

As the mic is brought within one inch of the program source, it picks up the low frequencies better than highs. This is known as the proximity effect. It's great for a female singer, who wants more guts or punch from the PA. All she has to do is bring the mic right up to her lips. Backing off will thin out the tone. But an acoustic guitar is difficult to mic. Low-gain mics must be placed closer to the source. When the mic gets into the resonating pattern around the guitar hole, the mic and system feed back at the hole's resonance. Couple this with the proximity effect and the guitar resonates within the low-frequency response range. The problem is now multiplied by the square, not just doubled. In practice, all mics fall short of the ideal, emphasizing some sounds at certain frequencies and limiting others

Response curves show how the response of the mic has been tailored. Some mics are built with a slight high-frequency boost that adds crispness to the sound. Others may have a switchable bass rolloff, meaning that the bass frequencies will be cut down a bit. A piano needs a mic that is sensitive to the highs and lows of the widest frequency range. A vocal mic will not do a very good job since it is most sensitive in the midrange.

About 40 years ago it was discovered that a boost in the 2,500 Hz to 4,000 Hz range would make a vocalist seem louder and stand out from the backup music without actually being much louder in electrical output. This high-frequency boost is called presence boost. Some microphones are designed with this type of proximity effect built-in.

Omni vs. Uni

An omnidirectional microphone has a sealed chamber behind the diaphragm so that sound pressure can apply force only to the front of the diaphragm. No matter from what direction the sound originates, as the pressure waves pass, the diaphragm will be subject to the push and pull of the varying sound pressures. The advantages of an omnidirectional microphone are:

1. For a given price, an omnidirectional microphone generally has a

smoother frequency response than its cardioid counterpart. Such smoothness of response is important because any roughness invites feedback.

2. An omnidirectional microphone is significantly less susceptible to breath pops than its cardioid counterpart.

3. An omnidirectional microphone is significantly less sensitive to mechanical shock than its cardioid counter- part. It is more rugged.

The first microphones were not very good at the high end. This was the result of a large diaphragm and the large box behind the microphone. A large diaphragm does not operate well at the high frequencies and a large microphone rear housing will cast a shadow in the highs arriving from the rear. Modern omnidirectional microphones have diaphragms less than one inch in diameter and correspondingly small housings.

Cardioid microphones have a highly directional pattern. They are usually more expensive than omnis, but have a significant advantage. These microphones can increase operating distance by a ratio of almost 2:1. This reduces the potential for feedback and is likely to decrease room reverberation and background noise. Cardioids are likely to produce a higher sound level before room feedback, especially when high levels of direct speaker sound reach the microphone from the sides or rear. With a regular omnidirectional microphone, the maximum working distance from the sound source (singer's mouth, guitar, trombone) is about 10 inches; the cardioid microphone will allow the source to be 18 to 20 inches away. It will produce a higher sound level before feedback.

Polar Pattern

A polar pattern is a graph of the ability a microphone has to pick up sounds originating in a different direction from the principal axis of the mic. Omni-directional microphones have equal sensitivity to sounds regardless of the direction. Cardioid microphones have unique polar patterns. Refer to the figure below for an example of the polar pattern of the Shure SM-58. This shows the loss in output (in dB) experienced as a constant-output sound source moves 360 degrees around a fixed

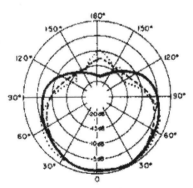

Fig 6.6 Polar pattern

microphone at a fixed distance. A unidirectional pattern looks like an apple with the stem at the microphone. An omnidirectional may be represented as an inflated balloon with the microphone at the center.

Microphone Selection and Placement

Microphone selection and placement greatly affects the sound of a recording or live mix. Even if your tape recorder and mixer are the best available, the final result will be poor unless you choose and place the microphones carefully. Each microphone sounds different, and it is important to select the microphone that gives the best sound for a given situation. The frequency response and polar pattern are two of the crucial specifications.

Flat-frequency response mics tend to sound natural. Mics with emphasized high-frequency response sound brighter with more treble. Microphones that roll off below the range of the instrument minimize room rumble. Mics that roll off low frequencies within the range of the instrument tend to sound weak in the bass.

Most condenser mics have an extended high-frequency response, making them suitable for cymbals or other instruments requiring a detailed sound, such as acoustic guitar, strings, piano and voice. Dynamic mics have a response good for drums, guitar amps, horns and woodwinds.

The polar pattern of a microphone affects the amount of ambience and off-axis sound that the mic will pick up. Omnidirectional mics pick up the most peripheral sounds, unidirectional mics are easier to target. The more ambience that is picked up along with an instrument, and the more an instrument's leakage is picked up by other mics, the more distant that instrument sounds. An omnidirectional mic must be placed closer to an instrument than a unidirectional mic to reproduce the same sense of distance. However, omnis tend to have less handling noise and breath popping than unidirectionals. In addition, the proximity effect bass boost of many unidirectional mics does not occur with omnidirectional. The bass boost may be a desirable effect with tom-toms or vocals.

The number of microphones used in a given situation varies greatly. Many ensembles (such as marching bands, choirs, string quartets) can be recorded using just two mics. An orchestra, a vocal group with many soloists, or a rock band may require multiple microphones for instruments or sections.

When using a hand-held microphone, it is important to use a wind-screen to eliminate explosive breath sounds and keep out saliva. Holding the microphone close to the mouth is a necessity with the ideal position, in front, even with the nose, and pointed down into the mouth. If the actor is at a podium, the usual position is in front of the actor and pointing up toward the mouth as close as possible. Sometimes using two microphones pointed in towards the actor from the sides is efficient. The primary rule in all microphone placement is to get the microphone as close to the source as possible for the cleanest sound and keep the number of microphones to a minimum.

The general rules to avoid feedback are:

1. Minimize the number of microphones. Each additional microphone adds potential for feedback. The choice may be between having a few microphones at high gain or a lot of microphones at a lower gain.

2. Keep microphones as close as possible to the desired sound source. This requires less gain in the mixer and therefore reduces the chance of feedback. Close miking also decreases the amount of leakage.

3. Try to keep sound sources on-axis, especially sources that radiate loudly. Some microphones add off-axis coloration. Boundary mics have almost no off-axis coloration.

4. Keep unused mics off whenever possible. If there is not any sound to be amplified, then it is not necessary to keep the potentiometer up.

5. Use a unidirectional mic whenever possible. It reduces the amount of leakage and is less prone to feedback.

6. When positioning the house speakers, make sure they are down stage of all microphones. Any mic that is pointed toward a speaker will feedback very quickly.

7. Use a direct injection box to mix electronic instruments.

To mic the following:

Vocals - in front of and even with the nose, pointed down into the mouth.

Instrument amplifiers - on short stands aimed directly into the speaker from about 6 inches to a foot away. Also split outputs, sending direct to one channel, miking to another.

Piano - use a PZM placed inside the lid in the center, or on the underside, or use two microphones, one for the high and one for the low end.

Horns - very close to the instrument, if not in the bell of the horn.

Leslie cabinet - upper part of cabinet to pick up sound of the rotating horn. Usually there is a big open slot at the back. Another mic at the bottom will pick up the bass frequencies.

Synthesizers - direct, or direct injection box.

Choir - mics placed with 3:1 rule. Thus, if mics are 4 feet above the heads, there should be 12 feet of separation between the mics. If placed 6 feet above the heads, there should be 18 feet of separation.

Acoustic guitar - at the center hole with the mic pointing straight at the hole at a distance of about 6 inches. Make allowances for the amount of room needed by the musician to play the guitar. Some acoustic guitars have pickups that allow the use of a direct injection box. This will yield the clean precise sound that is usually wanted with acoustic guitars.

Upright bass - low notes produced by the upright necessitate that the microphones be more sensitive to lower notes. In addition, because the string bass is played with one end resting on the floor, the mic can be attached to a short floor stand about six inches in front and pointed at the bridge or somewhere between the bridge and f-hole.

Woodwinds with reeds - these instruments employ a mouthpiece containing a reed. Most of the sound level escapes through the top five or six finger holes with a little left to radiate from the end of the instrument. Place the microphone either at the finger holes or at the bottom end of the instrument.

Woodwinds without reeds - flutes produce their sound when air is blown into a hole on the mouthpiece. Most of the sound originates near the mouthpiece so placing the mic near the player's mouth will give good results. Another technique is miking the flute approximately a third of the way down the barrel, pointing directly at the instrument from about two inches away.

Kick drum - drums are among the most difficult instruments to mic. The sound of a drum stick hitting a tom-tom or snare may overload a microphone. A good way to mic a kick drum is to remove the front head and place a pillow inside of the shell. This will reduce some of the resonance of the kick, creating a tighter sound with punch. A mic can either be placed directly on the pillow or on a stand facing the shell. Be sure that the chosen mic has good low-end response and is capable of withstanding sharp transients at high SPLs. If the drummer does not wish to remove the front head, try miking the drum from the back (batter or beater) head.

Snare drum and high hat - use a mic placed above the two to pick up both of the instruments. A condenser mic can be pointed downward on top of the cymbals. Snare drums can be miked with dynamic mics on top and bottom.

Mallet instruments - this is an interesting challenge. The ideal is to mic

each note on the keyboard, but this is impractical. A microphone about 18"
above will work, or use two mics, one each for the high and low ends.

Harp - place the mic on a short floor stand with a gooseneck or boom and
point it perpendicular to the sounding board near the middle to low strings.
An alternate method uses a small condenser mic wrapped in foam padding
and placed in one of the upper holes.

Practicum

1 Select an assortment of microphones from your inventory, place them
   on stands and connect them to a mixer that is amplified through loud
   speakers and monitor. Speak or sing through each mic in turn to hear
   what they sound like through the system. Listen for proximity effect
   and frequency response characteristics.

2 To illustrate the importance of phasing, take two mics, one in each hand.
   While speaking into one, move the other away and then bring it close.
   Note that as you bring them closer together, the sound intensifies
   (provided they are in phase).

3 Unplug the connector of one microphone. Reverse the wires on pins 2
   and 3. Plug the mic back in. Repeat the experiment in #2. Notice that
   as you bring the two mics together the sound will cancel. There is also
   a response change that happens gradually as you are bringing them
   together.

7 REEL-TO-REEL TAPE RECORDERS

Although we live in the digital age, many theatres rely on reel-to-reel tape recorders for sound effects. Tape editing requires cutting and splicing the sound cues and inserting leader tape between them. The advantage is that arranging your cues with leader tape provides a visual separation. The sound operator can see that the sound effect is ready to go. Refer to the figure below for examples of six different 1/4" tape formats.

Six analog tape track formats

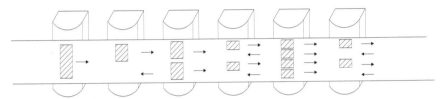

Fig 7.1 Analogue tape formats

Example 1. Full track recording: The magnetic flux produced by the head covers almost the whole surface of the tape. The entire tape is recorded in one direction only.

Example 2. Half-track monophonic: The flux pattern generated by the recording head covers less than half of the tape surface and the recording head is off-set to one edge of the tape. A monophonic signal is recorded on one-half of the tape and then the reels are inter-changed and the other half of the tape is recorded. The same half-track head is used for both passes. The tracks are, of course, recorded in opposite directions on the tape.

Example 3. Half-track stereo: Two recording sections (heads) are used to record two tracks simultaneously on the tape. Both channels are recorded in the same direction on one pass through the tape.

Example 4. Quarter-track, 2-channel stereo: Two record heads are used to record all four tracks on the tape. On the first pass through the tape, tracks 1 and 3 are recorded simultaneously. At the end of the first pass, the reels are interchanged and tracks 2 and 4 are recorded using the same two heads that recorded tracks 1 and 3. The actual program on the tape for tracks 1 and 3, and 2 and 4 is recorded in opposite directions, but since the reels are interchanged between passes, the tape is recorded and played in the forward direction for both passes of the tape.

Example 5. Quarter-track, 4-track/4-channel (quadraphonic): The head assembly consists of four separate heads and all four tracks can be recorded at the same time on a single pass through the tape.

Example 6. Quarter-track, single channel (Monophonic): The four tracks on the tape are recorded one track at a time. At the end of each pass through the tape the reels are inter-changed and the next track is recorded. The order in which the tracks are recorded is 1, 4, 3 and 2. Four-track recording gives maximum playback time, however, the benefits of stereo reproduction are lost.

Compatibility between various formats are as follows:

1. A half-track mono deck can playback a prerecorded full track tape.

2. A half-track stereo deck can play either a full track or a half-track tape but the signal from a half-track mono tape on side 2 will be played back in the opposite direction. However, the right channel output can be turned down and the left channel only used for playback of both sides of the tape. When playing a full track tape the left and right channel will re produce the same sounds.

3. A four-track stereo tape deck can play back both 4-track and 2-track tapes and from the point of compatibility has the widest possible range of utilization. When playing a 2- track stereo tape on a 4-track recorder, track #1 will be completely covered by the head. Track #2 will be slightly off alignment; but stereo can still be enjoyed by compensating for the slight loss of track #2 volume with the volume or balance controls of the amplifier. On the other hand, a four-track tape cannot be played back on a two-track recorder as both tracks #1 and #2, and #3 and #4 will be reproduced together resulting in mixed unintelligible sounds.

Almost all tape decks are designed and constructed to record and play back only one of the standard formats. A few 4-channel decks have a selectable 2-track playback head for compatibility with pre-recorded 2-track tapes. Full track and half-track monophonic decks for home use are rarely, if ever, available today. Full track professional decks may be purchased, however.

The gap between heads on multiple track recorders determines the highest frequency that can be recorded. For example, if the head gap is 0.00025," then divide the tape speed (e.g. 7.5 IPS) by the head gap to determine the frequency:

7.5 / 0.00025 = 30,000 Hz

Tape and Speed

Tape speed is measured in inches per second (IPS), referring to how fast the tape travels across the heads. Tape decks like the Otari MX 5050 have two speeds, 15 IPS and 7.5 IPS. Lower-end decks like the TEAC also may have two speeds, but in a lower range, 7.5 IPS and 3.75 IPS. Optimum performance is obtained at the higher speed. Noise reduction systems such as dbx type 1 are designed for use with 15 IPS decks.

The length of a full reel of recording tape, as well as the recording time, is determined by the reel diameter and the thickness of the base material. Running times for various speeds and lengths are listed on the back of most tape boxes.

Polyester base tape is preferred for use in humid or extremely dry areas. The use of 1 or 1/2 mil base tape is recommended for 4-track recording.

Record, Play, Erase Heads

Earlier models of tape recorders used a combined record/play head. With such a head, you cannot record and reproduce at the same time. Another disadvantage of the combined head was in the design of the width of the head gap. Modern head technology generally dictates that the gap width should be different between the record and playback functions for optimum output and frequency response.

When there are severe space and cost limitations, combined record/play heads are still used today. Open reel decks which normally have no head space limitations and usually command a higher price due to their special capabilities, normally have separate Record and Play heads. The separate heads allow monitoring of the tape during recording. This system has distinct advantages. You can verify that your tape is actually being recorded properly as you record. The playback signal can also be connected to the record head for special effects, such as sound-on-sound (simul-sync or self-sync), echo and sound-with-sound.

With separate record and playback heads there will be a time delay between the two heads and the tape speed. For instance, if the record and playback heads are 1 7/8" apart and the tape speed is 3 3/4 IPS, the delay is about 1/2 second. With the tape speed increased to 7 1/2 IPS, the delay is 1/4 second. At 15 IPS, the delay is about 1/8 second.

For some recording situations, even this fraction of a second is not acceptable. If a musician wants to add a new instrument or voice to a song already recorded and wants to listen to the recorded song for timing and synchronization, this delay would present a problem.

The erase head is located to the left of the record head in the deck. Its function is to purge the tracks of all previous recording by means of a strong alternating magnetic field immediately before the tape reaches the record head. This is done automatically whenever you select record mode in the deck.

Bulk erasure. This is the only satisfactory way to erase previously recorded 1/2 or full track tape to prevent undesirable "cross-talk" or chatter from the former material.

Bias and Equalization

In order to get the magnetic particles on a tape to respond properly to the changing signal supplied to the record head, a preconditioning bias is needed. Most home recorders today use an alternating current (AC) bias at a frequency of 50 to 150 kHz. This bias raises the magnetic level of the oxide particles so that even small changes in the signal from the record head will cause relatively similar changes in the magnetic level of the particles on the tape. Without this bias preconditioning, the oxide particles do not respond properly to the signal from the record head. This high-frequency bias signal is applied to the tape together with the desired audio signal by the record head. Since the bias signal frequency is much higher than the audio frequency range, there is little chance that the bias signal will interfere with the sound reproduction.

The amount of bias (bias level) affects the signal-to-noise ratio, distortion and the frequency response of the tape and hence of the deck itself. Too little bias will allow more distortion than is necessary. Bias also affects the output level of the tape. Normally, as bias is increased the signal level of the tape increases, up to a maximum output level which depends on the type and quality of the tape. Increasing the bias level beyond this point causes the output level (and consequently the S/N ratio) to decrease. The optimum level of bias is usually a compromise between the best results in S/N ratio, distortion, and high frequency response, and usually differs with different types and brands of tape.

The EQ selection must also match the type of tape formulation being used. If a deck was factory-adjusted for standard tapes and the recordist decided to use low noise/high output tapes with their accompanying high-frequency emphasis, the high frequencies would sound too bright. Most tape decks have a switch that can be adjusted to accommodate different types of tape, bias and equalization settings.

Simul-sync

Simul-sync, also known as sound-on-sound or selective reproduction, refers to using the record head to monitor the reproduced program. This enables a recording to be made on another channel synchronized (in phase) with the channel being reproduced. Since the exact sequence of selecting the simul-sync mode is peculiar to each tape deck, it is advisable to refer to the manual of the tape player before proceeding. Recording multiple channel synchronized material, like overdubbing sound effects onto a narrative poem or timing of instrumentals with rhythm sections, is made possible with simul-sync recording.

Time-code

Signals may be recorded on the tape to synchronize two tape recorders, or a recorder and another device like a video recorder (VCR). The Society for Motion Picture and Television Engineers (SMPTE) pioneered the use of a standardized timing reference in the film industry. A camera's film transport is locked by virtue of sprockets, but a time-code is needed to be able to synchronize video and audio tape to film and to one another. The most common is the LTC, or longitudinal time-code, placed as an audio signal on a spare audio track. In the synchronization process, a 1200 Hz modulated square wave is recorded onto a track using a time-code generator. A specially designed device or even a CD player may be used as a time-code generator. The code goes by the acronym of the Society (pronounced as "simp-tee"). There are different types of SMPTE signal depending on how many frames per second are used–24, 25, 30 and drop-frame.

A time-code reader is used to decode the information on the tape and display the data on a frame-accurate digital clock. A time-code synchronizer listens to the SMPTE data recorded on two or more machines, compares the time-code and adjusts the tape speed based upon the results of that comparison. The recorders are locked together by varying the speed of

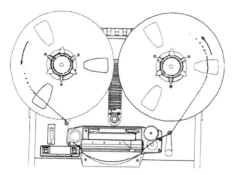

the motors. One of the machines is designated as the "master," the other is designated as the "slave." Its speed is continuously adjusted to maintain the desired relationship. These devices are connected to the tape decks by multipin cables.

Fig 7.2 Mechanical Tape Transport Mechanism

The European standard time-code is called EBU and is a 25-frame signal. There is also a time-code for MIDI (see Chapter 11), called MIDI Time Code (MTC). SMPTE-to-MTC and MTC conversion devices are available.

The figure above provides a typical example of the tape transport mechanism for the Otari MX 5050. It shows in basic diagram how the tape is threaded through the tape guides, across the heads, between the capstan and pinchwheel and around the tension arm. The mechanism for moving the tape incorporates two induction motors for the tape reels and a dc servo motor (direct drive) for the capstan. The capstan works in conjunction with the pinchwheel to move the tape across the heads. A pitch control is available to adjust the control range of the tape speed within $\pm 7\%$. The transport accomodates tape reels of 10 1/2 , 8, 7, and 5 inches in diameter in NAB or EIA hub configurations. In addition to the editing controls, a tape-splicing block is mounted on the head cover. Momentary-contact pushbutton switches on the transport are used to select operational modes: record, play, stop, rewind, fast forward, and edit. All of these modes except edit can be controlled from a remote location using an optional remote control unit.

Demagnitizing and Head Cleaning

The single most important point in tape deck maintenance is frequent and proper cleaning of the heads. The heads should always be cleaned before making important recordings and at least once for every eight hours of use. Dirty heads will cause a reduction in high-frequency response, irregular head wear, drop-outs and occasionally may cause the deck not to record at all. The small amount of time and effort required will be more than compensated for by the higher quality of recording and reproduction available if these procedures are followed.

Commonly used cleaning fluids are chlorothane, hydrogen peroxide and isopropyl alcohol. Be careful with these fluids since they may damage or corrode the head if not used properly. Some advise against strong solvents preferring instead to use a diluted mixture. Using a stiff cotton swab or a foam rubber wand, rub the entire head surface, being cautious not to scratch it. Repeat the process on each head until all discoloration and tape oxides are removed. Clean all metal parts over which the tape passes, such as capstan shaft, tape guides, tape lifters, etc.

During long periods of use, the heads may become slightly magnetized. As a result, high-frequency response will decrease, noise will develop, or in extreme cases, the high frequencies will dropout and noise will be introduced into the tapes. To keep the original fidelity, the heads should be degaussed (demagnetized) at least once for every fifty hours of use. Places specified for degaussing include each head, capstan shaft and guide post. Before proceeding with the following steps, move all pre-recorded tapes sufficiently away from the degaussing area.

1. Turn off power to the deck.
2. Turn on the demagnetizer device, bring the tip close to the head and slowly move it up and down four or five times.
3. Slowly move it away from the head
4. After finishing all points, turn off power to the demagnetizer only after it has been drawn at least twelve inches away from the heads.

Tape Storage and Handling

During playback, the biggest danger to the recording is a magnetized or dirty point on the deck, such as a head or capstan. Care for the tape must be continued even after playing by following these guidelines

- Protect the tape from dust. Keep it in the plastic bag in the original carton.
- Protect the tape from heat. Do not place it on top of audio components. Store it in a cool room but avoid freezing temperatures. Keep it out of direct sunlight.
- Protect the tape from stress. Tremendous pressure is builtup on the inner windings of tape. This pressure is acceptable unless you apply additional stress by bending or squeezing the sides of the reels. The problem is increased if the windings are irregular. Frequent starts and stops will cause uneven winding pressure and the tape will be unevenly wound from side to side

within the reel. Slight pressure on the sides will then break or crack the edge of the tape. Therefore, always prepare your tapes for longterm storage by rewinding them using the forward or reverse operating speeds. The fast forward and rewind speeds normally apply a greater tape tension that is not recommended for tapes that will be unused for a time.

• Protect the tape from strong magnetic fields. Just as a bulk erasure will remove the recorded material, so will a permanent magnet or the voice coil of a speaker destroy your favorite recording.

• Protect the tape from humidity. Fungus growths will cause irreparable damage to the tape if stored in damp places. Keep the tape in the original plastic bag, but insure that it is dry before storing.

8 COMPACT DISCS, MINIDISC AND DAT

The compact disc was invented by Philips N.V., a company with headquarters in The Netherlands. It was first marketed commercially by Sony and has revolutionized the way we listen to music. Compact discs are capable of reproducing sound that seems to emerge from total silence, with a dynamic range in excess of 90 dB. The compact disc has become the medium of choice for recorded music and sound effects. The first commercial units were shipped in 1983 and by the end of the decade CDs had supplanted cassettes and records. The "LP" is considered a relic of the past and is difficult to find in your local music store. However, you will find vinyl records in specialty stores in cities like New York, Los Angeles and London. Although contemporary dance club music and oldies are on vinyl, we have relegated turntables and cartridges to Appendix B.

There were only 45,000 CD players sold in 1983. By 1987 retail sales of compact discs reached the $1.5 billion level. As of March, 1988, there were 7 million CD players and 90 million turntables in American homes, but in that same year there were twice as many CDs shipped as vinyl records. Eight years later the statistics revealed that there were 780 million CDs sold in the USA (population about 260 million), which means 3 CDs per inhabitant. Europe has about 600 million people and CD sales of approximately 670 million.

How It Works

Refer to Figure 8.2 to see how a compact disc is played. The disc itself consists of billions of pits arranged in spiraling tracks. A low-power laser pickup shines a beam through the transparent plastic surface layer of the disc and focuses it on microscopic pits on the information surface. The pits, which represent binary digits (bits) of digitally encoded music, are 0.1 micron deep, 0.5 microns wide, 1.6 microns apart and 1 to 3 microns long. A 3-beam pickup system doesn't actually have three separate lasers, but a single beam of laser light split three ways. The center beam reads the data, while the leading and trailing beams monitor the position in relation to

Fig 8.1 Tascam CD-450 CD player

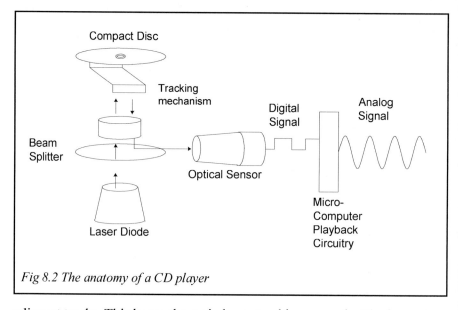

Compact Disc

Tracking mechanism

Digital Signal

Analog Signal

Beam Splitter

Optical Sensor

Laser Diode

Micro-Computer Playback Circuitry

Fig 8.2 The anatomy of a CD player

adjacent tracks. This keeps the main beam tracking properly. The laser plays the compact disc from the center of the disc to the outside edges. The revolutions per minute (rpm) change as the laser moves. The disc spins at about 75 rpm near the center and 300 rpm on the outside. As the disc rotates, the laser beam alternately falls onto pits and blanks between them. When the beam strikes a pit, light scatters; when the beam strikes a flat surface, light is reflected back to the pickup. Thus a series of pulses is produced and sent to the processing circuits for eventual conversion back to sound.

A CD's digital information is read as a stream of bits which is designed to be sampled 44,100 times per second (a 44.1 kHz sampling rate) with a 16-bit resolution. The two channels of a compact disc can reproduce frequencies within the 20 Hz to 20 kHz range with a signal-to-noise ratio in excess of 90 dB and total harmonic distortion less than 0.005%. To prevent ultrasonic noise from affecting the audio range of frequencies (below 20,000 Hz), a filter must be used to screen out unwanted signals. Early CD players used analog filters with very steep cutoff slopes. Unfortunately, frequency phase shifting caused by such filters made these CD players sound harsh, especially noticeable on cymbals, strings and brass instruments.

The latest generation of machines uses advanced digital circuits which filter out unwanted noise before the signal is converted back to analog. A technique called "oversampling" reads the incoming data at two or four times the standard rate, thereby suppressing the frequencies immediately above the audio range. Because oversampling shifts any residual noise to a much higher frequency, a very gentle final filter can then be used after analog conversion.

Because a CD is read as a stream of sequential bits of data, if a portion of the stream is missing or corrupted, so will be the music. Very sophisticated circuitry has been developed so you won't hear the errors. As the stream of data is read, each sample is compared with the one before and the one that follows. Too great a difference between samples indicates an error. By knowing what comes before and after the error, the CD player's brain can interpolate what is missing and fill in the gap. This error correction circuitry is so good even damaged discs can usually be played without degraded sound quality.

BMG has developed a digitizing process known as 96/24 that uses a sampling rate of 96kHz with a 24-bit capacity. The first CD released using this process was Bartok's Concerto for Orchestra created from a 1962 recording by Erich Leinsdorf and the Boston Symphony. It is expected that this digitizing process will be the standard for DVD audio recordings, since DVD players can play back that mode, but no CD player can do so.

Data is transmitted using the AES/EBU (Audio Engineering Society / European Broadcast Union) digital audio standard, probably the most popular digital audio standard today. Most consumer and professional digital audio devices (CD players, DAT decks) that feature digital audio I/O support AES/EBU. AES/EBU is a bit-serial communications protocol for transmitting digital audio data through a single transmission line.

S/P DIF (Sony/Philips Digital Interface Format) typically refers to AES/EBU operated in consumer mode over unbalanced RCA cable.

Manufacture

The disc actually consists of three layers—the disc itself made of transparent plastic; a reflective aluminum information surface; and a lacquer coating for protection. The physical representation of electronic pulses are impressed on the aluminium information surface.

The manufacturing process consists of the following:

1. **Editing**. A master tape, one of ten or so in existence, arrives from the recording studio. Three employees spend three to four hours in sound proof rooms editing the tape for digital recording.

2. **Laser Cut.** The tape is taken to two workers who create a glass master copy by exposing a glass plate to a laser beam controlled by a computer that reads the digital recording. The laser stores sound by burning tiny pits in the glass surface. These pits—a 10,000th of a millimeter deep—are read as music by compact disc players.
3. **Matrixing.** The glass master is put in a plating system to make a metal master and stampers.
4. **Molding.** The stampers are placed in injection molding machines. A plastic or high-grade polycarbonate resin is added, and the machine creates—one at a time—thousands of transparent copies of the master. The resulting discs are 1.2 millimeters thick and 120 millimeters wide.
5. **Coating.** A very thin (3 to 4 millionths of an inch) layer of aluminum coats the mold's pitted surface. This layer reflects the compact disc player's laser. Then machines add a protective layer of ultraviolet curing resin.
6. **Printing.** A few employees run machines that silkscreen labels onto each disc.
7. **Finishing.** The discs, stacked on spindles, are packaged automatically in thin, 6-by-12 inch boxes for retail sale.

PC makers began offering CD-recording drives in the early 1990s. This technology was available much earlier, but a dispute between record companies and electronics manufacturers delayed mass distribution. Things changed in 1992 when Congress approved an agreement between the recording and electronics industries requiring audio CD recorders and blank CDs to carry a matching electronic code. Recording cannot be done unless the recorder finds the CD's code. Now you can burn your own CDs with a CD recorder. Artists and record companies receive a 3% royalty from sales of blank audio CDs and a 2% royalty from the sale of CD burners. The U. S. Copyright Office administers the claims which must be filed by the artists in order to receive any money. Songwriters and composers receive one-third of the royalties, record companies and artists receive two-thirds. The loophole is that there is no royalty code required for CD burners on PCs because no one thought that they would be used for music. Now music enthusiasts are downloading MP3 songs from the Internet and burning CDs at the desktop. You can record the sound cues for your shows on a CD using your own PC burner.

MiniDisc

The MiniDisc (MD) format stores about the same amount of stereo audio as a compact disk. The MiniDisc uses a magneto-optical digital recording medium similar to the format originally developed for digital cameras and other data storage applications.

Fig 8.3 Tascam MD-301 mkII MiniDisc Recorder

The MD format has been available since 1992. Although the data rates for MDs are significantly slower than CDs, the MiniDisc has an elegant scheme to compensate for the lossy reductions. The MiniDisc

Fig 8.4 Sony MiniDisc

will record up to 74 minutes of audio onto a 2-1/2 inch diameter disc. There is a convenient jog dial for track selection and data entry. The text entry functions permit you to name the tracks which is perfect for theatre applications. You can name your tracks to correspond to your cues. The editing functions are also a big advantage since you can trim, combine, split, move and edit using A-B erase functions. You can move tracks (cues) around and the unit will automatically re-order the sequence. The sampling converter is used to convert the different sampling rates (i.e. 48 or 32 kHz) over to 44.1 kHz sampling frequency used for Compact Discs, MiniDisc, and DAT.

The rack mount Tascam MiniDisc unit above has many advantages for theatrical use. The audio connections available includes balanced and unbalanced analog I/O and digital I/O on S/P DIF optical connections so you may digitally record sound effects direct from CD or DAT. The portable unit below from Sony is handy to use in the field to capture original sounds or you can move it easily between theatres for recording and playback. The discs are slightly more expensive than blank CD-R discs, but you can record and edit your sound effects, rearrange cues and access selections randomly. There is a similar format called MD DATA that uses the SCMS (Serial Copy Management System) so there

Fig 8.5 Tascam MX-2424 24 track 24 bit Hard Disk Recorder

are no digital outputs. This is to prevent second-generation digital copying, so be wary when you are shopping for a MiniDisc recorder.

Participants in a comparison test at the 1998 USITT conference ranked the MD format along with CD and above Hard Disk recordings. The Tascam MX-2424 hard disk recorder above is a 24 track hard disk recorder having the capacity to record roughly 45 minutes across all 24 tracks of 24 bit audio to the internal hard drive.

Digital Audio Tape

Digital Audio Tape (DAT) represents another advance in electronic sound recording and reproduction. A DAT deck is a combination of many technologies, including a sampler's input electronics, a playback circuit that functions similarly to a compact disk unit and a cassette system that functions like a tape player or VCR. It utilizes special ultra-fine metallic pigments developed specifically for helical-scan recording, similar to the recording process in video decks. DAT is available in 40, 60, 90 and 120 minute cassettes. DAT has a dynamic range of 96 dB and an absolutely flat-frequency response from 2 Hz to 20 kHz. The signal is recorded in digital form at a sampling rate of either 44.1 kHz or 48 kHz. If a CD player provides a digital output in addition to the analog line output, it is possible to make an exact digital-to-digital recording from the CD to the digital audio recorder, provided that the sampling rates are identical. The Tascam unit below supports recording and playback at 32kHz, 44.1kHz, and 48kHz. The digital audio interface includes S/P DIF I/O on coaxial lines, with selectable SCMS code. SCMS code can limit distribution of your recordings with digital subcodes. The ability to override SCMS allows you to copy your own works as often as you wish.

DATs have extreme data density, recording a PCM-encoded signal that is similar to video. There is a rotating head and a mechanism to pull the tape out of the cassette for recording and playback (which means you can't switch out a DAT as quickly as you can an audio cassette). The tape moves slowly, about 1/3 of an inch per second. The input section has filters, sampling circuits and large-scale integrated circuits along with an analog-to-digital converter (A/D). The DAT's performance depends upon the same factors that affect the quality of sampling keyboards: sampling frequency, quantization rate and

Fig 8.6 Tascam DA-20mkII

input filters. The DAT standard calls for 16-bit linear quanitization, just like a CD. This is as good as most samplers, allowing for 65,536 signal levels with a dynamic range of over 90 dB. With a digital-to-digital connection, you can make an exact copy of any CD with a DAT recorder. The CD standard sampling rate is 44.1 kHz, but many DAT players offer a sampling frequency of 48 kHz.

On tape, a DAT signal is recorded in two overlapping bands. Error correction is part of any digital audio system. There is also subcode data for access and indexing information such as the beginning and end of selections, track numbers and elapsed time. Many decks allow you to add subcode data after the audio data is recorded, so you could add time code information for example.

Legislation had been proposed by large record companies to restrict digital audio tape recorders. It would have required an anticopy chip developed by CBS to be inserted into every DAT recorder sold in the United States. Its purpose was to prevent the making of digital tape copies from compact discs. Manufacturers were withholding DAT from the U.S. market, believing that the device would hurt the quality of the product. A report from the National Bureau of Standards supports this opinion. Critical listeners had perceived a change of tone in selected passages of music. This was attributed to phase shift in a key frequency, a phenomenon largely confined to piccolos and glockenspiels. David Ranada, technical editor of *High Fidelity*, found evidence of impaired reproduction. A sustained note in the last chord of the cantata in Prokofiev's *Alexander Nevsky*, after the Battle on the Ice and the rout of the Teutons, revealed flaws when played back on a protected DAT. Now all legislative efforts to put the system in DAT recorders have been curtailed.

Panasonic is one manufacturer that continues to produce professional machines such as the portable SV-250 for field and location recording, and the rack-mount SV-3500 for studio and permanent applications. The portable DAT weighs just 3.5 pounds, has an internal battery, mic/line inputs and 64-times oversampling digital filters. The studio version has high-speed search, full programming functions, multiple repeat mode, XLR ins/outs and a CD/DAT digital interface.

DAT holds the promise of noiseless recordings, sound effects emerging from total silence and instant access of recorded material. However, there are limitations in using DAT for theatrical applications. Since the digital recording is on a tape medium, it takes too long to advance the tape during fast cue sequences. DAT tape is more suitable for pre-show, intermission and background sounds such as extended storm or sea sounds. In a well-equipped theatre, the DAT machine might be used in combination with CD, tape or Minidisc.

9 EQUALIZATION

An equalizer is a sophisticated tone control, a more selective way of adjusting bass and treble. EQ is the quick way to say "equalization." There are many reasons why we use equalization. EQ is used to improve tonal quality and balance the range of frequencies according to the Fletcher-Munson effect. It also compensates for deficiences in the environment or perhaps a piece of equipment that has limited frequency response. Equalization can be used for special effects and to reduce noise and leakage. But the most important function of EQ is to shape the sound to satisfy the artistic demands of performer, designer and audience.

Equalization affects tone quality by boosting or cutting selected frequency bands. It alters the frequency response curve of the signal. Tone quality is affected by a change in the level of any portion of the spectrum. An equalizer raises or lowers the level of a particular range of frequencies. A boost in the highs makes instruments sound bright and crisp. A boost in the lows adds warmth. Too much bass makes the sound boomy. If you "roll-off" or cut the mids, you lose intimacy and presence.

An equalizer is described as either peaking or shelving depending on how it affects the frequency response. The figures below show a graphical representation of this principle. With a peaking equalizer set for a boost, the shape of the frequency response resembles a hill or peak with the highest distribution of frequency boost at the center of the bell-shaped curve, tapering off on either side of the target frequency. With a shelving equalizer the shape of the frequency response resembles a

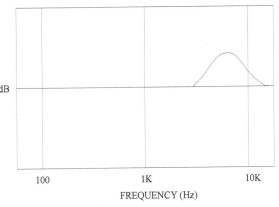

Fig 9.1 Peak equalisation

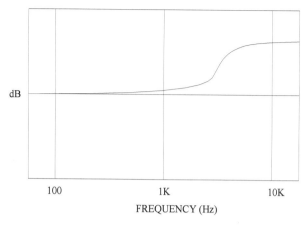

dB

100   1K   10K

FREQUENCY (Hz)

Fig 9.2 Shelf equalization

shelf, boosting all frequencies equally above the selected threshold.

Equalization controls on the mixer itself often allow areas of control over the audio spectrum. Rotary pots may reflect a combination of parametric and variable capacitance tone controls for the high and low end. This is analogous to the conventional bass and treble controls providing 15 db boost or cut at 100 Hz and 10kHz. In theory we can graphically represent EQ and learn a descriptive vocabulary for the resultant effects, but you have to train your ear in order to become skilled in equalization. In the theatre circus skills require hand-eye coordination. In the sound studio it is hand-ear.

Graphic Equalization

A graphic equalizer has a row of slide potentiometers which divide the audible spectrum into bands (range of frequencies). When the controls are adjusted, the positions of the sliders indicate the resulting frequency response. A good graphic equalizer can fine-tune the way your speakers sound in your theatre and studio environment.

Graphic equalizers normally incorporate sliding potentiometers giving about a 12 dB boost or cut when required. A typical graphic equalizer will provide two full channels of 1/3 octave equalization in one unit. The Applied Research & Technology (ART) Model 355 has 20mm center detent sliders with a selectable boost/cut range of 6dB or 12dB, balanced XLR and 1/4" and un-balanced RCA input and output connections, adjustable high pass and low pass filters, variable input level controls and signal clip level indicators. It has thirty 1/3 octave ISO standard frequencies per channel. To understand the concept of 1/3 octave, just remember the following principles. If a frequency is doubled or halved, that represents one octave. For instance, 440 Hz is the

"A" used to tune on a piano. Therefore, 220 Hz is the first "A" below and 880 Hz is the first "A" above. Divide these octaves into thirds and you will realize what frequencies you

Fig 9.3 The Applied Research & Technology (ART) Model 355

are adjusting with a 1/3 octave graphic equalizer. One thing to remember with regard to graphic equalizers: when you are adjusting one potentiometer and attempting to cut or boost a range (1/3 octave) of frequencies, you are also adjusting the adjacent frequencies as well. Some graphic equalizers are better than others, but none will allow you to isolate frequencies the way parametric equalizers will.

Parametric Equalization

The electronic device having the most flexibility in adjusting the tones and frequency response of a signal is the parametric equalizer. All of the "parameters" of equalization are controlled: the frequencies you want to modify, the amount of cut or boost, and the bandwidth of the frequency you are filtering. Using a parametric equalizer, you can select the range of frequencies you want to adjust, then define the narrow band of sound that you really want without disturbing any adjacent frequencies. Parametric equalization is especially helpful in vocal reinforcement or in feedback situations. The gremlin frequencies can be isolated and cut to establish a consistent response pattern with maximum headroom.

The dbx 905 is a typical parametric equalizer. It has three center-frequency adjustable filters. The high end extends from 800 to 20,000 Hz, the mid from 200 to 5000 Hz, and the low from 20 to 500 Hz. The amount of gain or attenuation at the filter's center frequency is then adjusted using a rotary potentiometer. There are LEDs to indicate clipping at any key circuit point.

There are important differences between parametric and graphic equalizers. You can target a particular frequency with more precision with a parametric. There are often separate controls for frequency and intensity, the amount of cut or boost. Some parametric EQs allow you to vary the bandwidth. The result is shown in the graph below.

An advanced technique for equalization involves "sweep EQ."

Fig 9.4 DBX 905

First you boost the EQ gain to a robust level. Then you "sweep" the desired filter to "tune in" the frequency you want to adjust.

Parametric equalizers have variable filters, but there are filters that serve as a form of equalizer. A filter attenuates frequencies above or below a certain frequency. For example, a 10-kHz low-pass filter removes frequencies above 10kHz. A 100Hz high pass filter attenuates frequencies below 100 Hz.

Setting EQ

The basic procedure in setting equalization parameters is as follows: First you should set your response curve flat and then adjust the approximate frequency range. You can apply full boost so the effect is easily audible. If it sounds bassy, turn it town. Fine tune until you reach desired tonal balance. Set a sweepable equalizer for extreme boost to find the problem frequency ranges (e.g. the feedback frequencies), then cut by the desired amount. There are absolute measures of frequency response that you can use, such as real-time analyzers and automatic equalizers. Although these techniques are often used by accomplished professionals, you should begin by taking recordings you are already familiar with and listen to them while adjusting the equalization settings. Listen to what

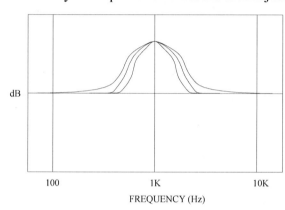

dB

100   1K   10K

FREQUENCY (Hz)

Fig 9.5 Varying the bandwidth

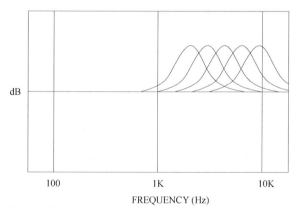

dB

100   1K   10K

FREQUENCY (Hz)

Fig 9.6 Sweep EQ

happens as you make adjustments at specific frequency ranges. Some sounds may become more obvious and attract your attention. This is where you should begin your efforts in adjusting EQ levels. Low frequencies are very problematic because they consist of large waves that can build.

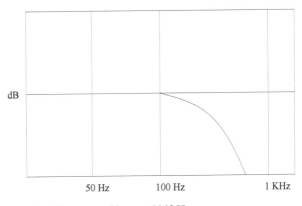

Fig 9.7 Low-pass filter at 100kHz

If the lows are overwhelming, roll of the low frequencies. You can be delicate with your touch since a few dB will make a significant change in the sound. As you set your values, you will see a curve taking shape in the pattern of sliders on your graphic EQ. Try to resist the temptation to make a visually smooth curve, that isn't always an indication that you've done your job correctly. Remember that in a graphic equalizer, each potentiometer also affects frequencies above and below the selected ones.

There are a lot of factors involved in setting equalization curves, but you must trust your intuitive powers as a sound designer, engineer or board operator in order to enhance the quality of the sound that you are trying to produce. The practicum exercises will help you develop those skills.

Practicum

1. Take turns adjusting each 1/3 octave pot on a graphic equalizer from flat to boost to cut. Become familiar with the tonal effect of each frequency band. Play individual tracks of instruments through it.

2. Use the parametric equalizer to sweep EQ and listen for resulting effect on the range of frequencies.

3. Create an EQ curve that simulates a telephone "person in a box."

4. Play a familiar piece of music through the EQ. Begin with a flat curve and then boost and cut frequencies to make it sound like it is on a boom box, car radio and concert hall.

10 SIGNAL PROCESSING AND EFFECTS

Signal Processors

Signal processors are devices that take a signal and modify it. There are three basic ways that a signal processor can change the nature of a sound. The first is to alter the amplitude of a signal. Compressors, limiters and noise gates adjust the amplitude. The second parameter that signal processors change is time. Reverb, delay, flange and echo are effects that modify or duplicate the signal over time. The third parameter has to do with the frequency spectrum. Equalizers (which also affect the amplitude of a signal), pitch changers and harmonizers alter and shape the frequencies present in the source signal. Noise reduction units are also components that increase the dynamic range and reduce the noise of the medium.

Noise Reduction

Noise reduction units such as Dolby and dbx are components that have substantially improved the quality of sound in the theatre by reducing the noise of the medium (tape, for instance). The first effective noise reduction was developed by Ray Dolby primarily for tape recording. The Dolby system requires that the tape carry a calibrated reference tone for adjusting the threshold of the circuit. In playback this reference tone is used to set the playback level. The Dolby system scans the audio program and increases the volume of the passages and sounds that are identified closest to noise producing and lowest in level. Dolby encoded and expanded material stands out clearly from the background. Dolby operates primarily on quiet passages since high level passages do not need noise reduction because the program masks the noise. There are three types of Dolby noise reduction. Dolby A is used for professional applications. It divides the spectrum into four separate bands which are then compressed and expanded independently. Dolby A reduces noise by 10dB below 5kHz and up to 15db at 15kHz. Dolby B costs less and was designed for cassette decks. It is effective on the high frequencies and reduces tape hiss by approximately 10 dB, thereby raising the headroom. Dolby C was developed to increase

Fig 10.1 dbx Model 150X

the effect by essentially doubling the noise reduction to 20 dB. Dolby is fully dynamic, it requires accurate playback and level control to be effective.

Where Dolby is a dynamic system, dbx differs from Dolby in that it is not frequency or dynamic range sensitive. It is a compander system, compressing the program during recording and expanding during playback. The dbx Model 911 is a typical example. It uses dbx Type I noise reduction for professional quality tape recorders. It doubles the dynamic range of the transmission medium to greater than 115 dB. Depending on the individual channel noise of the medium, it can reduce the noise of the medium 40 dB or more. This is achieved by compressing (encoding) the signal at a 2:1 ratio and applying a carefully tailored frequency response pre-emphasis during recording, and then expanding (decoding) the signal at a 1:2 ratio with a precisely complementary deemphasis during playback. The patented RMS detection makes the system virtually immune to phase shift related tracking problems. The companding is linear over a 100 dB range and requires no pilot tones or special calibration.

The dbx Model 150X is a single unit with two channels each of encode and decode Type II. There is a front panel bypass switch for each circuit. The 140X doubles the dynamic range to maximum of 115dB for typical limited bandwidth media such as cart machines, telephone/PTT lines, videotape audio tracks, and low bandwidth digital systems. The detector pre-emphasis in Type II is greater than in Type I, which causes additional gain reduction at high frequencies.

Type I is to be used only on tape machines with flat-frequency response (± 1 dB from 20 Hz to 20 kHz) and running at 15 IPS or greater, with full headroom maintained at high frequencies. Type II was developed for media where the high-frequency response is not as flat and headroom is reduced because of tape saturation or with broadcast audio equipment. The two systems are incompatible because the filters and pre-emphasis used in the rms detectors are different

The benefit of the 2:1 ratio compression is that the signal becomes easier for any medium to handle. Its dynamic range has been cut in half, with the hottest levels considerably reduced and the softest passages boosted. On decoding, the signal is precisely expanded back, and the original dynamic range of the program is retrieved without hiss, saturation distortion, or degradation of frequency response. There is none of the noise buildup normally encountered in transferring information from one recorded medium to another. Noise present in the original, naturally, is not reduced in this process.

Although simple in theory, classic 2:1:2-compander noise reduction could not be achieved before the development by dbx in the early 1970s of two patented circuits, the Blackmer rms detector and the voltage-controlled amplifier (VCA). The former enables optimum decode tracking and transient response despite the phase shifts typically induced by tape recorders. The latter affords precise gain control over an extremely wide dynamic range while maintaining very low noise and distortion.

With today's hotter tapes and faster meters, there are no longer any hard and fast numbers about maximum recording levels with dbx noise reduction. Generally, recording levels should always be as high as is consistent with clean sound. This means that peaks almost invariably should go well above the deck's nominal 0. In some cases peaks may go above +3, the end of the meter range for many decks, depending on the dynamic range and the spectrum of the program material. Synthesizer, female chorus, brass, percussion, music with considerable high-frequency energy, transients, and the greatest peak-to-average ratios, will require close attention to the meters and more prudent settings. But electric guitar, chamber music and small-ensemble jazz, piano, strings, male vocals, and any material that has been limited or compressed beforehand may usually be put on the tape at healthy, high levels.

Don't forget to mark the tapes "Encoded with dbx I," or "Encoded with Dolby C," since undecoded playback of encoded tapes or decoded playback of unencoded tapes is not much fun.

Digital Reverb and Delay

Early versions of digital delay, such as on 60's recordings of the Beatles, used tape loops. You can hear a primitive form of digital delay by recording two identical tracks on a tape recorder, playing them back using the normal playback (reproduce) head for one channel and the record head as a reproduce head for the other channel. You can use the record head as a playback head if your tape recorder has a self-sync or simul-sync function. What you will hear is one track played through the record head and the other played through the reproduce head which may be more than an inch away. Depending on tape speed, that gap can create a substantial delay to your ears.

A reverb unit simulates the sound by generating random multiple echoes that are too numerous and rapid for the ear to resolve. The signal is reproduced over time and the interval yields the "echo" effect which can simulate different environments and rooms from a concert hall to a small room.

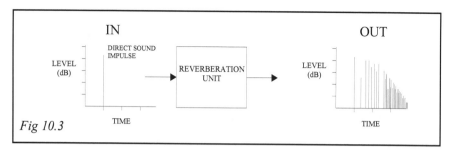

Fig 10.3

The delay unit accepts an input signal, holds it in memory, then plays it back after a short delay from 1 millisecond to a second. The delay is the interval between input and repetition. If we delay and then combine the delayed and undelayed signal, we hear two distinct sounds, the signal and the repetition, which is called an echo. Multiple echoes give instruments or voices fuller, stronger textures. Doubling occurs if we delay between 15 and 35 milliseconds. Chorusing and pitch bending occurs if we modulate a randomly swept signal. Flanging is what happens when we use a comb filter to sweep the signal. Flanging is especially effective on cymbals and gives a swishing,

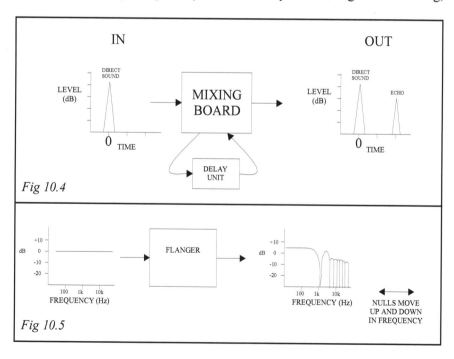

Fig 10.4

Fig 10.5

ethereal quality to the sound, as if music is played through a length of pipe.

Fig 10.6 The PD-3 digital delay from Applied Research & Technology (ART)

Another place where delay occurs is in the large concert hall. Remember that sound takes exactly one second to travel 1130 feet. Outdoor stadium shows must use digital delays for the speaker towers at the back, so that the audience does not experience unintelligible delay from the stage.

The PD-3 digital delay from Applied Research & Technology (ART) is designed primarily for time synchronization in multiple sound distribution systems for sound reinforcement, recording studio and loudspeaker time alignment applications. The PD-3 is a 1 input, 3 output delay. Each output is individually adjustable in precise 1 millisecond increments to a maximum of 255 milliseconds via front panel DIP switches. Via an internal switch, the PD-3 can be set to short delay mode. In short delay mode, the PD-3 allows for delay increments of 31 microseconds to a maximum of 8 milliseconds. Short mode is primarily useful for loudspeaker time alignment. The application will dictate the mode to use. All input and outputs are actively balanced assuring hum and noise free interfacing with other equipment. Connections are accomplished via both barrier strip and 1/4" Tip/Ring/Sleeve phone jacks on the rear panel. Internally the PD-3 uses a 16 bit linear D/A converter that meets the most stringent of audio performance demands. The audio signal is sampled at a 64kHz rate, allowing for a full 20kHz bandwidth. A crystal controlled timebase assures delay accuracy and long term stability.

Compressors/Limiters

Dynamic range is the difference in dB between the highest and lowest volume levels in any audio program. A compressor is a device that squeezes that dynamic range. The compression ratio is the ratio of output level change to input level change measured in dB. In a conventional compressor/limiter, normal program dynamics are heard until the input level rises above a preset threshold. At this point, the gain suddenly begins to be reduced by a fixed ratio. A compressor with a ratio of 2:1 would modify a signal so that a change in volume of 2 dB at the input would only change by 1dB at the output. Most compressors allow you to vary the compression range from 2:1 to possibly 20:1 or more. One of the applications is to smooth out variations in microphone level for voice, percussion or amplified bass guitar. When the distance between a vocalist and a microphone changes, variations in signal level occur. If the compressor is adjusted for low compression (around 2:1), these variations can be smoothed. The same can be done for musical instruments. Often the dynamic range is affected by the proximity of performers to the microphone. Bass tones often seem to disappear at low levels. A compressor can rectify this problem by pulling up those instruments that are hard to reproduce. Compression lessens the loudness variations among the strings and increases the sustain. Other instruments, such as horns, vary in loudness depending on the note being played, and benefit similarly.

With programs of widely varying levels, compression can prevent recording levels from saturating tape tracks. Compressors are frequently used to prevent excessive program levels from damaging drivers in sound reinforcement systems. There are many similarities between compressors and limiters. A limiter is a compressor with a high compression ratio, usually 10:1 or higher. A limiter begins its operation only above a certain input level called the threshold. The dynamic range of the signal is unmodified until it reaches a certain threshold above which the signal is compressed at a high ratio so that it doesn't get louder. Some models do both, compressing the signal up to a threshold after which it is limited. Most models have controls for setting how quickly the unit responds to the input signal. Limiters and compressors can also be used on the overall mix, often to keep recorders, sound systems and transmitters from overloading on loud passages. Limiting also benefits intelligibility by allowing low-level input signals to be reproduced through the system at higher volume. In a musical performance, this provides additional intimacy as the vocalist's whispers are heard clearly at each seat in the house.

As a general rule, the compressors should be as close to the amplifiers as possible in the signal chain. If the compressor is placed before the EQ, for example, a potentially damaging boost in EQ won't be seen by the compressor and the speakers may be damaged.

The compressor works by providing a gradual increase in the ratio of gain reduction as the input signal approaches and exceeds the preset threshold. Either peak detection or the more desirable rms detection can be used in compressors. For example, the dbx 903 acts as an rms-based absolute limiter at a compression ratio setting of infinity:1, and holds program material at or below a fixed output level. At settings beyond infinity:1, the 903 actually reduces the output signal whenever the input level exceeds the threshold setting. With

Fig 10.7
dbx 903

infinity+ compression an apparent dynamic inversion can be achieved, making the 903 capable of producing unusual special effects with percussive signal envelopes. Threshold sensitivity usually falls between -40 dB and +20 dB. The compression ratio can also be adjusted from 1:1 (no compression) through increasing ratios until infinite compression. The output gain is controllable from -20 dB to +20 dB, allowing the output level to be increased or decreased as necessary.

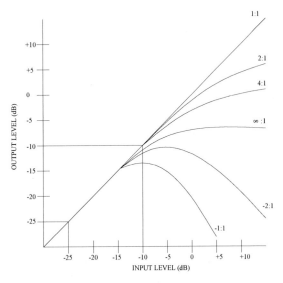

Fig 10.8 Compressor/limiter output curves

Range Expanders

A range expander increases the signal fed into its input by a given ratio. Expanders are the opposite of compressors and limiters. It can exaggerate the dynamic range of a signal rather than reduce it. An expansion ratio of 2:1 means that for a 1 dB change of level at the input, a 2 dB change of level appears at the output of the expander. An expander can restore some of the dynamic range lost in a compressor earlier in the signal path. It is important that expansion does not begin below the noise level of the system. Expansion, limiting and gate functions are sometimes combined on one instrument

Aural Exciters

Quite a few years ago a man named Curt Knoppel was building a stereo tube amplifier. Once completed, he found one channel to be working perfectly while the other sounded strange. For no apparent reason, he connected the "bad" channel to the "good" one and found that it enhanced the original signal. The Aural Exciter was born.

The first model introduced to the public also used tubes, and it was not sold,

Fig 10.9 Aphex Aural Exciter 104

but rented by the minute. Back in those days, recordings were made in acoustically dead studios where everything was closed-miked. Mixdowns were made to quarter-inch tape, at 15 IPS and usually with noise reduction. Aural excitement, added at the disc-mastering stage, brought life to mixes that seemed dull and/or lacking ambience.

Basically, the process is a combination of phase and amplitude distortion that, when added to a track or mix, does what EQ alone cannot do. An Aural Exciter is a psychoacoustic processor that increases brilliance not by equalization, but by adding harmonics not present in the original sound. Inside, a variable high-pass filter is used to roll off all frequencies below 1 kHz. In the process of filtering, a certain amount of phase shift and harmonic distortion occurs. After the filter, the signal is sent to a limiter that distorts in a musical way and makes the signal peaks seem louder. This is now called a harmonics generator because it generates musically related harmonics. The processed signal is now mixed back with the original, creating an enhanced effect that tickles your ear in a psychoacoustic way. The signal seems louder, but it is not. Because a high-pass filter is used, the sound is brighter across a wide frequency spectrum.

The result is a perceived increase in mid- and high-frequency response. This is not the same as boosting certain parts of the frequency spectrum with EQ, nor is it similar to inserting a high-pass filter in line. You do not hear evident boosts at certain frequencies. Aural excitement increases intelligibility, enhances stereo imaging, and creates increased presence and clarity.

By extending the harmonics of your audio path, the Aphex Aural Exciter 104 is able to restore the natural brightness, clarity, and presence that may have been lost during analog conversions or "Less-than-perfect" audio equipment. The Aphex 104 also may help when you are duplicating audio tapes. Practical uses for an aural exciter are easy to find. In the studio, it can be used at any stage from tracking to mixdown, or afterward to improve the sound of cassette copies. In a live situation, the exciter could be used to add an extra presence to a poor guitar sound, or just to improve the overall sound

Fig 10.10 dbx 902

of the entire mix. It could also save high-frequency drivers from being destroyed. It is recommended for anyone looking for the extra "zing" in their sound.

Warning: The exciter will also enhance certain high-end recording noise such as tape hiss. It does its job no matter what the program material might be. One suggestion is to use noise reduction in the signal path to defeat the potential problem.

De-esser

The dbx 902 de-esser makes it possible to achieve the desired amount of de-essing, regardless of variations in signal level. Using patented dbx® sibilance detection circuitry, the 902 compares the RMS energy of signals above and below a specified crossover point to precisely detect undesirable sibilance.

Noise Gates

The basic purpose of a noise gate is to remove unwanted background sounds in the spaces between desired foreground sounds. Note that there has to be some real level distance between the unwanted and wanted material – at least a few dB-in order for the noise gate to "get its foot in the door." If levels are too much the same (because of compression, for example), the downward-expansion efforts of the unit will go for naught. Therefore, use noise gates *before* any compressors.

A noise gate may be used to prevent or reduce leakage among microphones in live-sound reinforcement and during panel discussions. Placing a unit on each mike and setting its threshold below the level of the music or speech will achieve this. It can also be used during a remote interview to attenuate the noise from wind or air conditioning.

There are many possibilities for noise gates in a recording studio or on stage. Sound engineers can clean up a buzzy drum kit, or keep a closely miked piano track from being "contaminated" by leakage from a second instrument (e.g., a

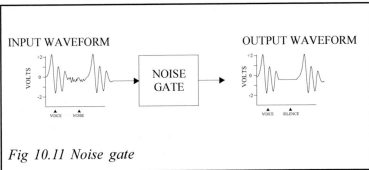

INPUT WAVEFORM   OUTPUT WAVEFORM

Fig 10.11 Noise gate

Fig 10.12 dbx 904

drum). This potential leakage applies to each drum in the kit. By gating out such leakage, a noise gate on each microphone will help it pick up only direct sound. The result is a tight, close-up sound from each individual drum.

A noise gate, like the dbx 904, is a very fast, voltage-controlled, below-threshold downward expander. It senses the level of an input or a keying signal and determines whether this level is below the front-panel threshold setting. If so, the signal gets attenuated; if not, it passes at unity (0 dB) gain. The amount that the signal is attenuated is a function both of its own level and of the settings of the attenuation, limit, ratio and threshold knobs.

As with other dynamic-range manipulators, nothing educates the user like thorough experimentation. "Hands-on" familiarity with this device will prove invaluable.

Digital Effects Processors

A digital effects processor uses highly refined LSI (large scale integration) technology to create natural reverberation. It is an electronic device that may have several effects stored in memory (ROM, or read-only memory that can't be changed by the user) as well as the capability of designing your own effects and storing those in memory. This is accomplished by selecting a preset effect and adjusting the parameters to suit your requirements.

The Yamaha SPX-90 is a moderately priced digital multi-effect processor that contains 30 preset effects comprehensive enough to suit most studio and performance applications. It also allows the user to create up to 60 additional effects and store them for instant recall. The SPX-90 can create effects far beyond reverberation. A variety of echo, delay, and special effects, each with comprehensive parameter adjustments, can be accessed at the touch of a switch. As the SPX-90 is MIDI-compatible, it can be programmed to apply separate effects to a number of MIDI-compatible instruments. It is useful in a variety of situations: acoustic, electric, PA, MIDI instrument and home recording systems. To ensure that user programs are not lost when the power is turned off, a built-in long-life battery acts as a backup. In normal use, the

Fig 10.13 DMV-Pro

battery will last five years, but it is advisable to change the battery before this time has elapsed.

The DMV-Pro from Applied Research & Technology (ART) is a stereo effects processor which all of the parameter editing, MIDI capability, and programmability of two full-featured effects processors for virtually all of the effects algorithms including hall, plate, chamber, and room reverb; chorus, flange, pitch-shift, tremolo, rotary, panning, phase-shift and delay options. Programming is quick and direct with dual LCD displays for each channel's parameters. Up to twelve parameters are available for each effect.

One hundred studio-crafted presets are available, with all 100 locations available for storing your custom sounds.

Sound Effects

There is a wide variety of sound effects available on record, tape and compact disc. The BBC sound effects library is a good place to start. There are also many other CD sound effect collections available. These are very clean, often recorded digitally as well as mastered. See the Product Resource Directory in Appendix E for the names and addresses of these sources.

You can always make your own sound effects. In Lily Tomlin's one woman Broadway show, *The Search for Intelligent Life in the Universe*, she worked extensively with her sound designer to come up with concrete sound effects: chains for the punk teenager, a hot-water bottle sloshing for a waterbed sound. The most effective means of creating customized sound effects is by working together with the artist to create the ideal sound for the dramatic context.

11 MIDI, SAMPLING AND COMPUTERS

The MIDI Interface

As keyboardists struggled with the headaches of integrating growing stacks of instruments into a single controllable system, some instrument designers recognized the need for a control signal interface standard for digitally-based musical instruments which would enable a musician to control one or more instruments from a master controller. A standard was formally proposed by Sequential in 1981. By the summer of 1982 several manufacturers had agreed on a modified form of the proposal, and the musical instrument digital interface (MIDI) was born. Instruments from two different manufacturers were first MIDI-ed together in January 1983. Since then, the MIDI scene has been growing explosively, and with few serious glitches. This has spawned the development of specialized performance controllers and sequencers. It also encourages the use of computers with synthesizers. Musicians have access to a multitude of new software packages for composing, score-writing, and sound synthesis.

MIDI is essentially a communication language that enables various digital devices to communicate with each other. MIDI allows devices to communicate by converting their actions into a language that can be transmitted by wires connecting the devices. The MIDI language, as with almost all other digital devices, uses the binary system as its codes for communicating. These binary codes (called bits) are transmitted at a very high rate of about 31,250 ($\pm$1%) bits per second (Kbaud). Because the data is transmitted at such a fast rate, it permits musical devices to communicate in real time, allowing practically instant communication and response between the devices. The hardware and software standard was initially created for live performances but has been used extensively in studio and composition environments.

Each MIDI-equipped instrument usually contains a receiver and a transmitter. Some instruments may have only one or the other. The receiver receives messages in MIDI format and executes MIDI commands. It consists of an opto-isolator, Universal Asynchronous Receiver/Transmitter (UART), and other hardware needed to perform the intended functions. The transmitter originates messages in MIDI format and transmits them by way of a UART and line driver. The interface operates asynchronously, with a start bit, 8 data bits (D0 to D7), and a stop bit. This makes a total of 10 bits for a period of 320 microseconds per serial byte.

The MIDI data generated by one instrument is sent to others as serial data over a single line. In serial data transmission, the bits are sent one after the other rather than simultaneously (requiring more wires). The bits are then received and collected in groups to be converted to a message or command by the receiving devices.

The MIDI codes or bits are not the actual sounds created by the instrument in digital form. They are a representation of the mechanics of how the sound was created. The actual sounds produced by the instrument are provided at the "line out" terminal and are completely independent of the MIDI network. MIDI codes do not recognize or care what the sound was that created them, MIDI cannot attempt to classify sounds since an infinite number of sounds exist. MIDI codes allow musical devices to respond to the actions of other devices and be driven by their commands. For example, if two keyboards are connected by a MIDI line, one of the keyboards can drive the other and make

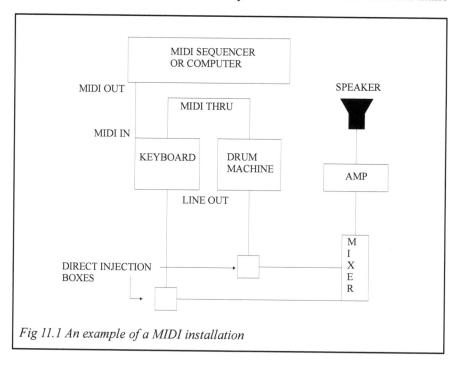

Fig 11.1 An example of a MIDI installation

it create sounds without actually touching the second keyboard. The sound created by the second keyboard is not dependent on the sound produced by the first keyboard, but reveals what the first keyboard would sound like if it had the second built into it.

In MIDI, details such as whether the key, or note, is turned on or off, or the position of the levers and switches and the patch/program settings, are sent over a wire in digital form.

MIDI commands are composed of three bytes of eight bits. Each byte has its own purpose. The first byte of a MIDI command is called the status byte. It contains information such as "note on" or "note off," channel numbers, real-time controller changes, program changes and more. Each of the different commands has its own unique arrangements of 0s and 1s. The second byte is a data byte and contains information such as the key number if the status byte is a "note on" byte. The third byte is also a data byte with more detailed information relating to the status byte.

MIDI connections are made by attaching the MIDI devices through MIDI lines which consist of five wires with 5-pin DIN connectors on the ends. The figure above shows a typical MIDI configuration.

Sequencers

A sequencer is a word processor for music. It is a computer-based device that accepts as input the data transmitted by any MIDI keyboard or other controller. Once inside the machine, the data can be altered, played back, or stored in permanent form. Computers can create MIDI data from software packages and play that data on any number of digital instruments. This allows entire compositions to be created and performed from a computer keypad without ever touching a synthesizer or instrument. The QY700 is a 110,000-note MIDI music sequencer with 32 tracks for recording instrument parts and 16 pattern tracks for assembling accompanying drum, bass and chord backing from the music database. It also includes a wide range of song, measure, track and event editing functions, high resolution and enough memory to hold up to 20 songs.

Cakewalk is a software program for the

Fig 11.2 QY700

IBM from Twelve Tone Systems that turns the computer into a sequencer. Columns display track, channel, event time in bar/beat/clock format, event type, and up to three data fields associated with the event type. These fields may contain information as to pitch (octave number), velocity and duration. Channel information includes such things as note-on and note-off, pitch bends and after-touch. System information includes start, stop, continue, timing clocks, and song position pointers. The computer is connected to a MIDI-equipped keyboard or other instrument. Interface hardware is needed to send MIDI signals through the computer. The MIDI specification requires a current loop serial interface. There are MIDI interfaces available for most computers.

One of the first examples of MIDI in action was the 1987 tour by the rock group Chicago. The tour, dubbed the "MIDI tour," was appropriately named. The band used small devices that converted analog signals to MIDI data. These were linked to a large computer/MIDI network behind the stage. Every instrument on stage, except for the vocal mics, was connected to this computer network. At the center of this system were two computer operators who sat in front of computer terminals "directing traffic." Massive sampling data storage systems and memory units were connected to the computer system. The result of all of this was that the audience almost never heard the actual instruments. Instead they heard samples of studio recorded instruments stored in the network. The computer operators were able to completely change the sound of every instrument after each song.

Lighting manufacturers have incorporated MIDI features into their systems. With MIDI, lighting chase rates can be synchronized to a clock. Cues may be programmed into the lighting console and then the console can be treated as a MIDI channel device. A MIDI-event will trigger light cues just as it may initiate an audible event. As a memory tool, MIDI is incredible, but it hasn't been used in full-blown touring applications for lighting yet. Perhaps this is because MIDI consoles are limited to 32 channels currently. Many software designers for lighting control consoles are becoming familiar with MIDI and we should see more innovative products before too long.

Synthesis

Robert Moog's name has been a household word among musicians since his groundbreaking work with voltage-controlled synthesizers in the 1960s. By 1975, the synthesizer scene, such as it was, was dominated by ARP instruments and Moog Music. Roland and Korg were just getting started while

Oberheim was sliding into the packaged synthesizer market with its expander modules. In an article for the first issue of *Contemporary Keyboard*, Robert Moog defined what a synthesizer is. At the time, most people, even most keyboardists, didn't know. The answers, which were developed in succeeding issues, had to do with oscillators, filters, and amplifiers. There was no worry about microprocessors or channel assignment modes. In those days it was taken for granted that an electronic keyboardist should be able to follow a patching diagram or a computer program flow chart. But in 1975, performing keyboardists were just starting to feel comfortable with simple synthesizer controls. However, the history of synthesizers owes as much to the vagaries of business as it does to technological breakthroughs or inventive geniuses. Without a doubt, the foremost of these breakthroughs is the proliferation of the microprocessor.

A microprocessor is a digital integrated circuit that contains all the computation and program execution circuits needed to implement a small computer or digital controller. Equipped with the right object code (i.e. operating programs), a microprocessor is capable of performing many sophisticated tasks inside an electronic musical instrument: keyboard scanning, parameter assignment, envelope and modulation waveform generation, automatic oscillator tuning, and so on.

In the early 1970s, Keith Emerson used a ribbon controller for both musical expression and theatrical gesture. Now musicians have touch-sensitive keys that are designed to allow the player to shape tones naturally. Key pressure can vary loudness, brightness, or pitch. Keyboardists are aware of the musical importance of responsive keyboards.

The Yamaha EX-7 music synthesizer has a 1-megabyte memory; expand up to 65 megabytes by installing optional SIMM memory modules with 512 preset voices which may be edited to create your desired sound effects, or you could create new original voices and save them to a floppy disk or external storage device. There are 6 knobs that can be assigned to control parameters such as pitch bending and and aftertouch response. Scene buttons can be used to

Fig 11.3 Yamaha EX-7

switch between memorized controller setups. The sample mode lets you "sample" sounds via a microphone or line source which can be mapped to and played via individual keys of the keyboard using the Key Map mode. It is also possible to sample directly from the internal tone generator system, so you can capture any sound you create and save it for later use. It is not only a synthesizer, but also features a wide range of sequencing functions. It has a 30,000 note memory for recording and can be synchronized to an external device using MIDI clock or MTC (MIDI Time Code).

Sampling

According to legend, the Fairlight was originally conceived in the mid–'70s as a harmonic and waveform synthesis system. Sound sampling was added, almost as an afterthought, when the designers discovered that their synthesis design included 95% of the hardware needed to sample sounds from the outside world. The Fairlight's success was due primarily to its sound sampling capability, which allows the user to musically manipulate any sound that can be recorded. Shortly thereafter, E-mu introduced the Emulater and Ray Kurzweil developed the Kurzweil 250 which included sounds in permanent memory ROM. Ensoniq's Mirage made basic sampling capabilities available at a bargain price.

In Chapter 1 we discussed the nature of sound waves and the regular pattern of peaks and troughs called frequencies. A single peak and trough pair is called a cycle, and sound is most often discussed in terms of the number of cycles per second, or Hertz (Hz). If a sound has 30 or 40 cycles per second, it is said to have a low frequency or pitch, and if 10,000 cycles are happening per second, it has a very high frequency. It is important to understand that sounds in the real world are not made up of simple, mathematically pure waves. A human being can listen to a woodwind quintet holding a sustained chord and tell without much difficulty which note is being played by the flute, which by the oboe, and which by the French horn. This type of analysis is still beyond the power of any computer program yet written.

When a sound is converted into fluctuations in electrical voltage using a microphone, the voltage fluctuations are smooth and continuous. The voltage is an analog of the air pressure: higher pressure, higher voltage. If the microphone is a good one, the voltage waves will resemble very closely the sound waves that gave rise to them. If the microphone is not a good one, distortion of the waves will occur.

Now comes the tricky part. When we've got an analog voltage that is fluctuating in a smooth, continuous manner, between 0 volts and +10 volts, let's say, it can have literally an infinite number of values, 3.1415926535 volts for example. The computer likes to see this number as a digital value, so we decide what increments the computer can handle. For example, if we are dealing with analog signals between 0 and 10 volts, we might decide to divide this range up into .01-volt increments. Each step (.03, 1.76, 8.20 volts, etc.,) would be assigned its own number for computer purposes. Now the computer is in an ideal position to take a "snapshot" of the voltage as it exists at a given moment in time and assign that voltage value to a computer number. The device that performs this operation is called an analog-to-digital (A/D) converter, and it is the heart of the digital sampling process.

One snapshot won't do much good because the voltage is constantly fluctuating. A short time later we need to take another snapshot, then another. In order to get any kind of a meaningful picture of the waveform, we need to take a lot of snapshots, or samples, and we need to take them very quickly. The speed with which we take samples is called the sampling rate. The basic rule is that the sampling rate must be at least twice as fast as the highest frequency to be sampled. If we want to sample sounds at 20 kHz, the sampling rate must be at least 40 kHz. That is 40,000 samples every second. Pro audio sampling rates tend to be slightly higher than this: 41.9 kHz, 44.1 kHz, or even 50 kHz. The Nyquist frequency is half the sampling rate. It refers to the highest frequency that a given device can safely sample.

Numbers are stored in digital memories as groups of binary (two-state) digits, called bits. Each bit in a sample accounts for a factor of two in the accuracy of a digital number. Thus, if a sample is recorded as an 8-bit number, that means the dynamic range of the input waveform is divided into 256 (two raised to the eighth power) possible levels, and one of those levels is recorded. Of course, audio waveforms vary continuously, so the process of dividing the sampled waveform into 256 levels introduces error. This error is heard as noise or as distortion. If you follow the math through, you see that each additional bit per sample reduces the error by 6 dB. For a bit sample, the error is 48 dB below the maximum signal. Most real-sounds instruments use 16-bit sampling. Some top of the line instruments use 32 or even 64 bits.

Computers

Sound control has been advanced with the utilization of computers. Futuristic special effects, once relegated to science fiction, are now commonplace. From simple programmable delays to effects processing and digital control, micro-processors are used for an increasing number of functions. The dawn of the digital audio workstation with a control computer as its brain is here with products made by Tascam, JVC, Studer and Sony. The new tools of the industry, as important as loudspeakers and microphones, are smart faders, back-lit LCD display windows, real-time equalizer/analysers, surround mixing and automation.

A computer interface for sound installations has been proposed using an RS-422 serial interface which would set an industry standard for digital control protocol. This type of interface allows control over great distances. The effective limit of the RS-232 standard, familiar to computer users already, is approximately 50 feet, whereas the RS-422 can be run nearly a mile. The interface will be capable of linking different types of computers and microprocessors, and the receiving equipment will let the sending unit know it has received the data. SCSI ports are used for data transfer between the computer and external storage or recording devices.

The special nature of theatre requires a variety of sources and locations for sound reproduction. The computer is ideal for flexibility of speaker selection, multiple inputs and remote control. Altec has developed a program called AcoustaCADD, which analyzes the elements of sound in an environment. Imagine interfacing this with other devices. Knowing all of the parameters of the sound system and room, the computer could adjust all of the appropriate levels of microphones and speakers as well as set delays and equalization for any microphone position chosen.

Some of the new products are unique and exciting. Oxmoor Corporation has a remote digital volume control system and digital control equalizer. An external Macintosh computer is used with trademark TWEEQ software for display of mouse-driven graphics. The software allows fast flipping between stored curves for A-B comparisons. T.C. Electronic of Denmark has introduced a combination graphic equalizer and spectrum analyzer capable of tracking feedback on a "search and destroy" basis.

Software designers are hard at work developing a library of "icons," representational pictures that graphically portray functions such as "increase loudness," or "stop tape," or "cut speaker #4." Prototype systems indicate that an operator will be able to select a location, such as stage left proscenium, with a mouse. Once the microphone is plugged into the selected location, the operator might use the computer to control and fine tune the microphone and loudspeaker characteristics to suit the venue.

Fig 11.4 Richmond Sound's AudioBox

The computer can electronically patch loudspeaker and amplifier configuration. When speaker lines are installed in new facilities, it is advisable to run a separate line for each receptacle location, rather than parallel multiple outlets. This will allow future accommodation of computer-selected output routing. The possibilities are limitless.

The digital signal processing chip (DSP) is ideal for analyzing or manipulating sounds. For instance, a soprano's voice is recorded in digital form via a microphone attached to the computer. The DSP chip stores her voice in digital form. Then you may play it back with CD quality or alter the voice in some other way.

Richmond Sound in Vancouver has developed a number of products beginning with the Command/Cue matrix in 1988 which used a PC with programmable crosspoint switches to control up to an astonishing 4,096 faders. This massive task is accomplished smoothly, quickly and effortlessly. It can execute an almost limitless number of cues of enormous complexity, including fades, loops, clock-timed follows, effects and pans. Richmond Sound's new interface called AudioBox, a versatile theatrical device which adds signal processing capability. You can use standard audio and midi software, a digital or automated console and run eight external and eight independent but synchronizable onboard sound sources to any of sixteen separate outputs with variable delay and EQ on all inputs and outputs. You can use it as a sound generator or distributor. It has the capacity to store 128 shows with a 2048 x 32KB size limit per show, but unlimited cues within the 32KB size limit.

Timing can be synchronized to stopwatch or MIDI time code. It has MIDI IN, MIDI OUT, MIDI THRU, and a SCSI port for transfer of randomly accessible show files. There is a 3.2GB hard drive for storage of shows and digital audio. You can combine it with editing software such as ABEdit for windows for basic programming functions.

Computer-controlled cueing

SFX is a software product that manages the execution of sound effects.

Basically, SFX allows you to control "wave" or "midi" sound files that you have stored on your computer's hard drive or audio tracks accessible through a CD-ROM drive. It will also control MIDI devices, provided your computer has MIDI output capability. Since SFX is a computer-based program, all of the effects you control must reside in files on either your hard disk or on a CD. Essentially, this is a product for the theatrical sound designer who is ready to replace or supplement reel-to-reel tapes, cassette decks, DAT players and external CD-Audio devices with computer playback of digital sound effects. Although computers are currently involved mostly in the "studio" phase of production, that is the gathering and editing of sound effects, SFX and other products utilize the computer for the "performance" phase, to prepare and arrange cues for execution during a performance.

One advantage of using a computer for sound effects is that the files are stored with descriptive names as a sound effects library that remains available for future productions. You can organize your collection of sound effects into different lists. For instance, you might want to keep one library of transportation sounds, another of human sounds. You select sound files from the list in and create cues with associated notes, time and labels. Status windows will maintain on-screen information about each cue, including act, scene and page as well as description. Cues are executed with the click of a mouse.

What kind of computer do you need to run sound cue software? The market is changing so fast that I'm reluctant to recommend a specific model. However, you should probably have a fast processor (at least 1GHz), a sound card and 20G of hard disk space. WAV files take up lots of memory. A CD-ROM would be handy, but not absolutely necessary if you have another way of acquiring sound effects such as a microphone or line input on your sound card.

SFX can also be controlled by MIDI Time Code. Stage Research produces another application, SFX Time Code, that reads and writes MIDI Time Code. Using MIDI Time Code, cues can be triggered by another MIDI device such as a lighting console, sequencer or MIDI instrument. SFX Time Code is not included with the basic SFX software but must be purchased separately.

I'm not so sure that we are ready to scrap all of our audio storage and output devices quite yet, but this product is very well designed for the Windows environment and accomplishes just about everything it claims to do. I was able to test the edit and playback features enough to realize that SFX would be very useful for anyone who relies upon computer-stored sound effects for theatrical production. This software package might even encourage someone to put together sound effects for a show using only digital sound files and computer control.

This chapter is still being written. Computers are being used now to control the movement of sound on stage by automatic panning and output selection. They are also being used as sequencers to control the output of multiple MIDI devices. Many mixing consoles contain microprocessor circuitry, small computers for automatic gain and EQ control. The digital amplifier is described in Chapter 4 of this book. Nearly every electronic device has the potential of benefiting from computer technology. The sound designer should be content with nothing less than a system that allows the creation of sound as a transparent extension of the artistic imagination.

12 LIVE SOUND REINFORCEMENT AND RECORDING

Mixers, microphones, loudspeakers, amplifiers, cartridge players, tape recorders, compact disc players, digital effects generators, equalizers, noise gates, harmonizers, reverb units, limiters and compressors are all eminently portable these days. Witness the quality and quantity of equipment touring into your local rock music venue. In the past, most of this gear would be available only in permanent studio settings. Today, a typical theatre is likely to have a full complement of touring gear as well as permanent playback and reinforcement equipment.

Many venues designate space for mixing consoles on the main floor of the auditorium among the last rows of orchestra seating. Often seats are removed expressly for this purpose. The necessity for the sound operator to hear the sound being mixed is crucial. For a live sound mix, the sound engineer should not be housed in a booth alongside the light board operator. While it is easy for the master electrician to see the effect of his work on the stage through a window, the sound operator must be exposed to the acoustical properties of the hall to do an appropriate mix, especially for live sound reinforcement.

The ultimate touring system these days most likely belongs to a "heavy metal" rock n' roll band. The PA system may fill several semi-trailers with as much as 25 tons of equipment including 200 sound cabinets. The 40,000 watts of such systems may be twice as powerful, per person, in a 10,000 seat arena than your average home stereo system. Monitor systems more powerful than main systems of a few years ago are designed specifically for band members to hear themselves play. The benefit to the theatre sound designer is that a substantial amount of equipment has evolved through the demands of the touring rock n' roll road show.

Microphone and Loudspeaker Placement

One of the problems with loudspeaker placement which has developed in concert situations, both indoors and outdoors, is the proliferation of foldback speakers for the performers. Often there are as many speakers provided for them as for the audience. Microphones will pick up all of this ambient sound unless properly positioned. To avoid having undesirable sound arriving at the mic and distorting the intended sound, it is important to use microphones with highly directional polar patterns.

Control of the stage monitor system is accomplished by providing a separate mixing console. Each musician may then control balance and EQ. The monitor sound engineer is able to listen to each musician's mix on his headphones using the PFL (pre-fade listen).

A typical main mixing console in an auditorium or theatre has between 16 and 48 input channels with 4 to 16 outputs and 6 to 8 effects sends. In an outdoor situation, the console would be located up to 100 yards from the stage. Large performing venues have more complex mixing systems with separate main and enhancement subgroups. Often vocals, effects and music are mixed via subgroups, then routed to stereo mains.

Singing, Instruments and Speech

Musicals and concerts require a big sound that modern audiences have come to expect. Composers, knowing that portable sound reinforcement equipment is as sophisticated and as readily available as that in a sound studio, write orchestrations to take advantage of the new technology. They are unfortunately encouraged by producers who equate loudness with excitement. As a result, actors may lose the ability to project because they rely on sound reinforcement too much to reach the back of the theatre.

Fundamental frequencies for intelligibility are from 500 to 5,000 Hz. Fundamental frequencies for singing range are as follows: bass, 75–340 Hz; baritone, 90–380 Hz; tenor, 130–480 Hz; alto, 190–640 Hz; soprano, 240–1,000 Hz. With a loud band behind the singer these frequencies can easily be overshadowed by the sound arriving from the instruments. Highly directional microphones like the Shure SM-85 or SM-58, have a roll-off at 100 Hz and 8,000 Hz and a 6 dB peak somewhere between 3,000 Hz and 5,000 Hz which make them good vocal microphones.

Vocals are almost always split from the instruments so that the loudspeakers used for vocals can be equalized to fit the requirements of the singer. The instruments can then be routed to their loudspeakers. This isn't always practical in a small theatre where loudspeakers are not as plentiful.

Electronic instruments may be routed to the mixer through a direct injection box. Since this eliminates the need for a microphone, there is no off-axis sound to worry about. Instrument amplifiers sometimes have an output sufficient to go directly into the mixer. Synthesizers, electric organs and guitars can use the direct injection box. Microphone inserts are also available for certain wind instruments, such as the flute.

In establishing the overall sound for instrument reinforcement, begin with the individual instruments and then the individual sections of the band or orchestra. Do the strings, brass, woodwinds, drums and percussion sections and then move on to the solo instruments, then the backup vocals and finally the lead vocalist(s). Clarity, articulation and balance are the objectives.

Use the rehearsal period to get rid of all feedback and set the proper levels. Try not to ride the fader except during the rehearsal period. Major changes should be noted on the sound plot or cue sheet. The essence of proper sound balancing is to use your ears and follow the sound plot. Do not over EQ. Begin flat and adjust only as necessary.

Psychoacoustics

Acoustics refers to the science of sound dealing with the propagation and transmission of sound waves. Acoustics describes the effect of various mediums, including reflection, refraction, diffraction, absorption, and interference, as well as the characteristics of rooms, theatres and studios. The elements and properties of acoustics are considered in greater detail in Chapter 13.

Psychoacoustics also considers human perception of sound. It begins with the ear and the process of using sensory apparatus to perceive or hear sound. Thus, it is necessary to consider not only the physical environment in which the sound is generated, but the location and predisposition of the listener. A good example of psychoacoustics in action is the loudspeaker demonstration room of your local audiophile store. The environment is usually well designed from the standpoint of comfort and listening pleasure, with on-axis directivity, well placed reflective surfaces and relaxing chairs or couches for the customer. This contrived environment may color your perception so that when the selected speaker is taken home to an apartment with linoleum, plaster, glass and beanbag chairs it sounds completely different.

The object of theatre acoustics is to project the sound of the performance out to the entire audience and to have it arrive everywhere with similar characteristics of spectrum and intensity and without excessive reverberance. The purpose of a sound reinforcement system is to present amplified but natural sound. Placement of the sound source may be anywhere on stage with the sound waves arriving at the listener's ears at different rates and from various paths. The stage and auditorium will absorb or reflect sound according to the architectural elements that are present. Since sound reflects around an enclosed environment until it is absorbed, or decays through loss of energy, the "hard" and "soft" surfaces play a big part in acoustics. Theatres for live stage performances are "live" or have a lot of hard surface area which reflects sound to overcome the absorbing qualities of a seated audience. Cinemas are designed to reproduce sound through loudspeakers, so they may have many "soft" surfaces. Each auditorium will have its own acoustic characteristics.

As in lighting, the angle of incidence of the sound wave equals the angle of reflection. Loudspeakers that coincide with the resonant qualities of the hall can double the range of frequencies. Noise from sources like air conditioning, stage motors, lobbies, rehearsal rooms, and greenrooms are considered undesirable masking noises and can interfere with the purity of sound in the performance space. Sound from traffic, aircraft, emergency sirens can also be annoying. Lower Sproul Plaza in Berkeley is a place where percussionists enjoy practicing due to the excellent reverberant quality of the concrete and buildings. Unfortunately, Zellerbach Hall sits on the same plaza. At least one performance of Marcel Marceau was delayed due to intermittent noise leaking through to the stage.

13 ACOUSTICS

Description

In the broadest sense, acoustics is the science dealing with sound. The chapter on waves considered many fundamental elements of acoustics such as frequency (Hz), response to tones and intensity. Subsequent chapters dealt with different methods of propagating, recording and transmitting sound and how to route and control the output. In this chapter, acoustics will be considered in a more restrictive sense. It is concerned with those qualities of a space that have to do with how clearly sounds can be heard in it. The focus is on the interaction between the environment and the source, and how it affects production, transmission and perception of music or speech. In an enclosed space, reflection, absorption and diffusion of walls, ceiling, floor or any solid objects may contribute as much or more to the sound than the direct path from source to listener.

Sound is created by materials that vibrate. Molecules of air are set in motion, producing an outward traveling wave. It may move for a few hundred or several thousand feet. Sound travels at 1130 feet per second in air. Sound travels much faster under water and at depth. Divers filming underwater volcanoes on the south shore of Hawaii, the "big island," encountered deafening sounds from the flowing rock that sent shock waves strong enough to move their masks. Of course, in the theatre, air is the primary transmission medium. However, today's audience does not sit on a hillside as in the sunny outdoor theatre of ancient Greece. Instead, carpet, glass, wood, gypsum board, air-conditioning, street noise and concrete surround the spectator and affect the sound waves that color the listener's perception.

The study of acoustic properties provides a means for analyzing how the initial vibration, whether it be from a loudspeaker cone, violin string or actor's vocal chord, travels through air, encounters interfering surfaces, is reflected or absorbed and finally reaches the critical listener's ear.

For an understanding of acoustics and definition of terms, it is necessary to turn to several important sources. The single best source for acoustics remains *Music, Acoustics and Architecture* by Leo Beranek. He completed a 6-year study of 54 concert halls in 1962. His findings presented physical data on the halls, along with the expressed preferences of many professional musicians, including conductors, performers and music critics. From this material he extrapolated those acoustical qualities that contributed most to the success of a hall and evaluated in numerical terms their relative importance. This research provided a way to evaluate acoustics. Another useful source is Dr. George C. Izenour's *Theatre Design* which is to theatre architecture as Beranek's book is to concert hall acoustics. Rollins Brook has contributed to the knowledge of acoustics and updated many of fundamental concepts in a chapter titled "Rooms for Speech, Music and Cinema," found in the *Handbook for Sound Engineers*. All of these sources should be consulted for a complete understanding of acoustics.

Myths

One of the persistent myths of acoustics is that there are no definite rules. However, the theoretical foundations of acoustics were established late in the nineteenth century by the English physicist Lord Raleigh. Later, Wallace C. Sabine, a 27-year old assistant professor, was approached in 1895 by President Eliot of Harvard to improve the acoustics of the Fogg Art Museum in Cambridge. His colleagues warned him that the problem was so complex that a complete solution was hopeless. After five years of research he gave to acoustics the classical reverberation equation and made the first advances in the application of acoustics to architecture. Before electronic equipment was invented, it was not possible to verify the data that Sabine produced. Once the amplifier, loudspeaker and microphone were available, acousticians were able to produce and accurately measure sounds consistent with Sabine's theory. Without these tools, previous designers of theatres and performing halls could only learn about acoustics by listening to past successes and failures, and speculating as to what was responsible for each. It is no wonder that the study of acoustics is surrounded with an air of mystery.

Among the arcane beliefs are that paint on the wall, gold leaf on the statues, wooden beams in the wings, or broken wine bottles under the stage will benefit the sound of a hall. As mentioned in the Introduction, the Greek theatre had excellent acoustics. But when the manager of a world-famous concert hall said that his hall had perfect acoustics because everywhere in it one can hear the sound of a pin dropped on the stage, Eugene Ormandy said: "I don't want to hear a pin drop, I want to hear the orchestra." Acoustics are not merely concerned with projection of faint sounds from the stage to the most distant seats.

Some other beliefs are that small halls generally sound better than large ones, that halls built to serve many principles are inferior to ones built especially for concert or opera, that a wooden interior is required for good acoustics and that old halls sound better than new ones. It has been proven repeatedly that excellent acoustics can be heard in a large hall. It is also a misconception that steel, glass and concrete cannot be used effectively. In order to keep the sound energy inside of a concert hall the walls are usually made hard and heavy. Of course, it may be necessary to add other absorptive materials in combination with reverberant ones to modify an environment to become acoustically effective for a variety of production modes. As to whether acoustics improve as the hall ages, that may have more to do with the reputation of a particular hall or the growing acceptance of regular patrons over a period of time.

Attributes

Following is a description of attributes originally suggested by Beranek in his investigation of musical and acoustical qualities:

Intimacy: Indicates to a listener the size of the room. It is not necessary that it be actually a particular size, but only that it sound as though it is. An intimate hall has presence. The listener's impression of the size of a hall is determined by the the interval between the sound that arrives directly at his ear and the first reflection that arrives there from the walls or ceiling. This interval is also called the initial-time-delay gap. In Beranek's study, intimacy was considered to be three times as important as any other attribute.

Liveness: A hall that is reverberant is called a live hall. A room that reflects too little is dead or dry. A live room is often said to be acoustically superior to a dead room. In most halls, seats that have poor sight lines also have defective acoustics. Room size has a lot to do with liveness. If the cubic volume is large for the size of the audience and the interior surfaces are sound reflective, it will be live.

Warmth: A hall may be live, but deficient in bass. Fullness of bass tone relative to the mid-frequency tone gives the impression of warmth. To state this another way is, a hall will have a warm sound if frequencies below 250 Hz have longer reverb times than the frequencies between 500 and 1000 Hz. A full, rich bass gives a warm sound. Too much bass is called boomy. If the lows have a shorter reverberation time, than the sound is said to be brittle.

Loudness of direct sound: In a small hall the direct sound will reach the back rows with adequate loudness. If the hall is too large, the effect of the inverse square law is felt. Intensity will decrease in direct proportion to the square of the distance. Loudness will then be too low by the time it reaches the distant listeners. Direct sound is usually at its best about 60 feet from the stage.

Loudness of reverberant sound: This is related to the intensity of the sound that does not travel directly to the listener and the reberberation time of the hall. It is inversely related to the cubic volume of a hall and upon total absorption.

Definition or clarity: A hall has definition when the sound is clear and distinct. A hall that lacks definition is described as blurry or muddy. This attribute is related to intimacy, liveness and loudness of direct and reverberant sound. It is a combination of four of the previous five attributes.

Brilliance: A bright, clear, ringing sound rich in harmonics is described as brilliant. It is affected by the initial-time-delay-gap. A hall that has liveness, clarity and intimacy has brilliant sound.

Diffusion: This attribute concerns the orientation of the reverberant sound in space. It is best when the reverberant sound arrives at the listener's ear from all directions in equal amounts. Irregular interior surfaces and long reverberation times will diffuse the sound. Diffusion will be lacking if a hall has smooth side walls and a ceiling which discourage cross reflections and scattering of the sound waves. Poor diffusion may result also when the stage area is reverberant but the rest of the hall is dead.

Other attributes are balance, blend, ensemble, texture, freedom from echo, freedom from noise, dynamic range, tonal quality and uniformity. Since these last nine attributes primarily apply to musical performance and not theatre, detailed descriptions are omitted.

Room Size

The enormous stone cathedrals of the middle ages, with lengthy reverberation times, were well suited for hymns and religious ceremonies. Since the Mass was celebrated in Latin, understood by few outside of the clergy, intelligibility was not an issue. The entire space, audience and stage, of Shakespeare's "wooden O" would have fit within the orchestra of Epidaurus. The relatively short distance between actor and audience, and the importance of the spoken word, made the Elizabethan theatre an ideal space for dramatic performance. The Guthrie Theatre is overall only slightly wider than the Greek *skene*. Max Reinhardt's Grosses Schauspielhaus was three times the size of the Guthrie, but not even half of Epidaurus.

Throughout history, composers have written with a particular space in mind. A perfect example is the music-drama of Richard Wagner written for the Festspielhaus in Bayreuth. The Redoutensaal in Vienna existed in Beethoven's time. It seated about 400 people and had a reverberation time with full audience of about 1.4 seconds at mid frequencies. Many of the larger halls of the nineteenth century had reverberation times over 2 seconds. Perhaps this was because music sounds louder in a hall that has long reverberation times, particularly in the rear of the hall. It enhances the bass.

Often a facility, especially on the university campus, is designed for multiple use including lecture, drama, dance, orchestra, musical comedy and cinema. Since music has a greater dynamic range and a greater frequency range than speech, the first step in designing a multi-purpose hall is to decide what will be the priority of the facility. Is it a concert hall, a road house, or a drama playhouse? If the choice is for the spoken word, then each time music is performed the reverberation time must be raised somehow. If the hall is designed for music, something must be done to lower the reverberation time for speech, which may then require a reinforcement system for sufficient volume and clarity. Since the impact of a concert or musical comedy often depends upon the loudness that the performing group can achieve, it is crucial to know that loudness varies with room volume and with audience size. These design factors must be taken into account when designing the performing space.

Initial-time-delay gap

A listener's impression of the size of the hall is determined by the initial-time-delay gap (ITDG), the interval between the sound that arrives directly at his ear and the first reflection that arrives there from the walls or ceiling. Fig 13.1 shows a graphic representation of the difference between the arrival of the direct sound and the arrival of the first reflection in a simple rectangular room. It is clear from this analysis that as the width and height of the hall change, so will the initial-time-delay gap.

The principle problem associated with a hall of large cubic volume is a too long initial-time-delay gap at the ears of many of the listeners. If the ITDG is as short as 19 milliseconds, the acoustics may be excellent. An ITDG greater

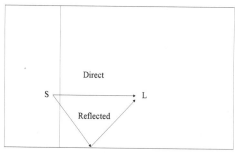

Fig 13.1 Time delay gap

than 49 milliseconds suggests an acoustic property that is less than adequate. Research has determined that the ITDG should be less than 25 milliseconds, or 25 one-thousandths of a second for clarity and intelligibility.

Corrective measures may consist of sound-reflecting surfaces hung hung horizontally between the ceiling and the main floor. Panels have been employed either to shorten the initial time delay gap or prevent the unfortunate focusing of sounds from curved ceilings, or to direct the upper registers of the strings over the heads of an audience seated on a flat floor to the listeners at the back. Reflecting panels were used as early as 1953 by Lothar Cremer in reconstructing the Herkelessaal in Munich. In 1954, Bolt, Beranek and Newman, Inc. used similar panels in Caracas, Venezuela and in the Kresge Auditorium in Cambridge, Massachusetts in 1955.

At the University of California in the early 1970s, an acoustic consultant was asked to retune Zellerbach Hall. A Real-Time Analyzer was used to determine which surfaces needed treatment. Then plaster was added or subtracted to create an ideal reflection/absorption pattern. The result was a subtle, yet effective change that revealed the violins in the orchestra much better than before. Today's designers and consultants are adept at using moveable panels to change the acoustics of a hall to suit the particular performance, whether it be drama, opera or symphony. Often these panels are electronically controlled and can be adjusted to tune the hall. New concert halls, such as the Performing Arts Center in Tampa, may have a combination of moveable panels, curtains and walls that can be altered for symphony, opera or drama.

More recently, a renovation at Carnegie Hall in New York revealed concrete under the stage. Concertgoers had complained that the hall did not sound as good after a renovation in 1985. When the floor began to warp, the discovery was made.

The current era is characterized by the implementation of variable acoustic systems, and electronics has replaced architecture as the controller of acoustics in some multipurpose auditoriums. Decoustics, a Canadian manufacturer of acoustic products, is one manufacturer of a system that electronically changes the acoustics of a space to suit different kinds of productions. Called the Acoustical Control System (ACS), it consists of an array of microphone and speakers controlled by a central processor. The sound as heard by the microphones is analyzed and the speaker output is modified to correct problems created by reverberation and absorption.

Reverberance

Reverberance is generally defined as the time required for the sound pressure level in an enclosed space to decrease 60 dB.

Reverberation depends upon:

1. the length of the reverberation time.
2. the loudness of sound relative to background noise.
3. the ratio of the loudness of the reverberant to the direct sound.

The direction of reverberation is also important, since early reflections off of side walls are now recognized as having a greater effect on intimacy than those from above or behind the audience. Later reflections should be perceived as arriving simultaneously from all directions. Reverberance is a major factor in liveness, loudness and clarity. Too little reverberance will degrade the first two attributes, too much will degrade the last.

Rooms designed for speech work best with a reverberation time less than 1.5 seconds, preferably under a second. Halls designed for music will have good acoustics if the reverberation time is slightly more than 1.5 seconds. A performance of Bach organ music or choral recitals will benefit from longer reverberation times. Lectures and drama will have better articulation with shorter reverberation times. Opera and musical comedy falls somewhere in between these two extremes.

Intelligibility

Clarity is the degree to which individual sounds stand apart. It is related to reverberation and background noise, including sounds both inside and outside of the hall. Therefore heat, ventilation and air conditioning will affect intelligibility as will traffic or machinery operated in the near vicinity.

The required conditions for the hearing of speech, according to Izenour are:

1. The speaker must speak loudly enough or his speech must be amplified.
2. The room must be free from noise and excessive reverberation.

3. The shape of the room must be designed so that it is free from echoes and interfering reflections in order to provide the optimal distribution of reflected sound to all listeners.
4. If the speech is not amplified, as is usual in a small auditorium or an intimate theatre, the speaker must face the audience or face nearby reflective surfaces that reflect speech energy to the audience.

Rooms should not be:
1. Afflicted with interfering or masking noises like heat, ventilation and air-conditioning equipment (HVAC).
2. Impaired with echoes or other interfering reflections.
3. Disturbed by focusing effects like concave surfaces.
4. So diffuse that it prevents localization and identification of the sources of sound on the stage.

Rooms should be contructed with:
1. Optimal dimensions and shape for the generation and distribution of sustained and impulsive sounds of early and delayed reflections.
2. Growth and decay characteristics that are adjustable between live and dead for speech and music.
3. Diffusion of reflected sound for low-, mid- and high-frequencies so that direct sound heard by the audience will beenhanced by successive reflections of the sound which will flow smoothly to the listener from all directions. This gives the audience the feeling that they are immersed in sound.

Absorption

Absorbing materials are used in acoustics to control unwanted reflections and to reduce overall reverberation time of the room. Absorption may be used to tune a room for speech or music. For good speech reinforcement the reverberation time should be uniform from 200 to 4000 Hz, although a small increase in reverberation time around 500 Hz is acceptable. Large rooms will show the effect of air absorption above 2000 Hz. There are three types of absorption:
1. That which is from construction materials and air inside the room.
2. That which is intentionally applied to surfaces.
3. That which comes from room furnishings, carpet and audience.

Air absorption is related to distance between the source and listener. Any absorption due to volume will have an effect on high frequencies above 2 kHz. There is a strong relationship between good hearing and good sightlines. In most halls, seats that have poor sight lines also have defective acoustics. Sound whose frequencies are above 1000 Hz (e.g. violin tones) do not bend around corners or obstructions. Remember that the wavelength of sound at 20 Hz is 56.5 feet and at 20 kHz it is 0.0565 ft (5/8 inch).

Reverberation time differs with the frequency coefficient of absorption. A greater value for this coefficient means more absorption. Carpet, velour, audience and empty seats are very absorbent relative to brick, glass and gypsum board. exactly how much more is indicated in the chart below which lists absorption coefficient values at various frequencies for each square foot of a selected material.

Absorption coefficients of selected materials (sabins per square foot) frequency						
Material	125	250	500	1k	2k	4k
Brick	0.03	0.03	0.03	0.04	0.05	0.07
Concrete block, painted	0.10	0.05	0.06	0.07	0.09	0.08
Carpet w. pad	0.08	0.24	0.57	0.69	0.71	0.73
Med velour	0.07	0.31	0.49	0.75	0.70	0.60
Wood floor	0.15	0.11	0.10	0.07	0.06	0.07
Glass	0.18	0.06	0.04	0.03	0.02	0.02
Gypsum brd	0.29	0.10	0.05	0.04	0.07	0.09
Plywood	0.28	0.22	0.17	0.09	0.10	0.11
Audience (ft²)	0.60	0.74	0.88	0.96	0.93	0.85
Upholstered seats (no aud.)	0.49	0.66	0.80	0.88	0.82	0.70

Carpets serve the dual purposes of floor covering and noise reduction. Noise reduction is achieved in two ways, carpets absorb the sound energy, and movement on carpets produces less noise than on bare floors.

1. Carpets laid directly on bare concrete had a noise reduction coefficient.
2. Fiber type has no influence on sound absorption.
3. Noise reduction increased as pile weight and pile heights increased. Cut pile has greater absorption than loop.
4. Pad material has a significant effect.

Normally walls are considered to be sound barriers, and the applications of absorbent materials to the walls of a room aid in the reduction of noise levels in a noisy space. While almost any absorption material may be used with success on walls, there is a certain class of material called wall facing or treatment specifically designed for this purpose. These generally have a fiberglass or mineral fiber core covered with fabric. They may be attached directly to the wall or attached by a system of furring strips to create an air gap between the treatment and the wall. As in the case of ceilings, this air gap would serve to decrease the low frequency absorption of the treatment.

Amplification

A general rule is that well designed rooms smaller than 25,000 ft³ will rarely need amplification (e.g. 20'wide x 50'long x 25'high). Halls larger than 250,000ft³ will always require amplification (e.g. 100'w x 100'l x 25'h)

The need for amplification in rooms for speech is determined by:

1. The level of background noise.
2. The level of the direct speech signal combined with the early reflections.
3. The level of the late reflections.
4. The difficulty of the message to the listeners.
5. The age of the listeners.

Another problem is too much amplification. Small proscenium theatres are often used for big-band or rock concerts that were probably never imagined by the building's designer. When the SPL gets ridiculously high and the building begins to shake, it is well past the time to reduce gain. If the sound level remains high, the best advice is to purchase a set of industrial ear plugs, preferably ones that will reduce the loudness by at least 20 dB.

14 SOUND CUES

Designing the Sound Plot

The process of creating a sound cue sheet involves a lot of planning and preparation. The first step is to obtain a script if there is one. Read through the script a couple of times and note what sounds are called for by the Playwright. Then, consult with the Director to understand his concept for the production. At this point, you may have some ideas and be able to make suggestions about environmental or atmospheric sounds, pre- or post-performance music for the audience, and any special effects. Make an input list of all of the sources to be used during the actual production such as tape players, turntables, compact disc players, microphones, cartridge machines or synthesizers. Before loading the show into the theatre, you must confer with the Scene Designer and Technical Director about loudspeaker placement and any on-stage practicals like a radio or phonograph. The Costume Designer also needs to know about any special requirements concerning wireless microphones, transmitters or battery packs. You must also work closely with the Stage Manager to determine where cues will be called during the show. It is important to call sound cues clearly and not confuse them with lighting or fly cues.

The preliminary sound plot will list all of the sound cues, but the actual levels and EQ will have to wait until technical rehearsal. This will also be the time when the cues are coordinated with specific lines or stage business. The final cues must be written in such a way that you can follow them at a glance, without having to read a lengthy narrative. Letters and arrows are the easiest to see, but numerical sequences are clearer when the Stage Manager calls cues over a headset. "B" and "D" sound similar through an intercom. "Sound cue #5" and "Sound cue #6" makes it perfectly clear. Refer to Appendix G for an example of a cue sheet.

Artistic and Technical Duties for Sound Personnel

The Sound Designer is an important member of the production team in the theatre. Working in collaboration with the director, scenographer and technical director, the sound designer must plan and prepare sound effects, music, live microphone and instrument reinforcement for performance. The sound design is not merely a matter of recording cues to be used in a show, but also includes determination of equipment to be used in recording and playback as well as the locations for mics, loudspeakers and occasionally even the mixing console.

The Sound Technician or Board Operator must assist the sound designer in the recording of sound effects for the show and become adept at operating the audio equipment. The Sound Technician must also rehearse and run the show, write a cue sheet and be able to execute the cues at the appropriate time in the proper sequence. This list is meant to be a guide for Sound Designers and Technicians in the theatre.

Sound Designer

1. Read the script, making notes on sound cues, atmosphere and music.
2. Meet with the Director and Scenographer to determine artistic requirements and apparent location of sounds.
3. Consult with the faculty sound advisor early in the planning process.
4. Attend production meetings with production staff to set schedule and solve problems.
5. Establish a calendar with due dates and deadlines.
6. Determine whether live mics or instrument reinforcement is necessary.
7. Decide which components will be used for recording, playback and reinforcement.
8. Select type and number of loudspeakers based upon dispersion and frequency response needs.
9. Select, arrange, record and edit all music, sound effects and live sound reinforcement for voice and instruments for the production.
10. Process or adapt stock sound effects or make effects not on pre-recorded sources.
11. Meet special requests by Director for sounds to be used in acting rehearsals prior to technical rehearsal.
12. Make back-up recordings of all sound used in the show.
13. Consult with scenographer and technical director on location and load-in of sound equipment including mics and loudspeakers.
14. Make sure all technical elements are in place and operable by the start of technical rehearsals.
15. Set levels while sitting in the house during rehearsals for sound effects and reinforced music.

16. Make sure that the Sound Technician records the proper levels for sources and outputs and that cue sheets are prepared accurately.
17. Set and review cues with Director and Stage Manager during rehearsals.
18. Alter cues as necessary.

Sound Technician

1. Meet with Sound Designer to learn sound requirements for the show.
2. Meet with the faculty sound advisor to arrange training.
3. Attend production meetings.
4. Keep a schedule of due dates and rehearsals.
5. Make sure you do not have any outside conflicts during the rehearsal and run of the show.
6. Arrange for access to sound booths and storage areas. Request keys if eligible from appropriate staff.
7. Learn how to operate all equipment used in the show.
8. Assist the Sound Designer in finding music and other sound sources.
9. Assist the Sound Designer in recording sound cues.
10. Make preliminary recordings for the Director to use in rehearsal.
11. Install and connect loudspeakers.
12. Secure loudspeakers with locks in areas subject to theft.
13. Set up live sound reinforcement equipment.
14. Determine quantity and placement of headsets and beltpacks needed. Notify staff charge of the inventory how many you need, when you need them and how long the show will run.
15. Make sure all technical elements are in place and operable by the start of technical rehearsals.
16. Instruct actors in proper use and handling of wireless microphones.
17. Make sure to use fresh batteries in wireless equipment for each performance.
18. Work with Stage Manager and Sound Designer to prepare cue sheets for called and visual cues. Make sure your cue sheets are legible.
19. Always arrive at least 1½ hours before curtain to set up and check out equipment prior to opening the house, but more prep time may be necessary if the show has lots of microphones or other special set-up requirements.
20. Start up equipment following proper procedure.

21. Check equipment and test sound levels before each rehearsal and performance. Notify Stage Manager that the sound crew is ready for the house to open. Do not leave the theatre prior to show time without the permission of the Stage Manager.
22. Operate sound during rehearsals and develop sound cues. Prepare clear notes about patching arrangements, pre-set volume settings for inputs and outputs, turn-on and turn-off procedures.
23. Keep all cue sheets stored with the show tapes. If it becomes necessary, someone should be able to run the show even if the original operator is unable to be present for a performance. Never keep cue sheets or tapes in your car, bookbag or at home during the run of a show. Find a locked cabinet to secure these materials at the theatre.
24. Take notes from Director, Stage Manager and Sound Designer, making changes as necessary.
25. Adjust levels compensating for audience size and noise level in consultation with Sound Designer and Director.
26. Set up intercom headsets for rehearsals and performance. Strike and set up each night when required.
27. Provide show mix to recording equipment if recording is being made for archives or video feed.
28. Shut down equipment following proper procedure.
29. Remove microphones and other equipment from locations subject to theft.
30. Strike sound equipment after final performance. Collect headsets, cable and beltpacks and return to storage.

Leader and Splicing

Editing tape is a way to make creative recordings by eliminating and joining different segments of a recording into one tape. Broken tape can also be easily mended by splicing, one of the steps required in editing. Leader, which is blank noiseless tape, may also be inserted to obtain timed spaces and clean leads into a cue.

Leader tape comes in paper or plastic form. Both are supplied on spools, 1000 feet for paper, 1500 feet for plastic. The 1/4"-width paper leader is 2.5 mil thick, plastic is available in the same thickness as the tape itself, usually around 1 mil. There are advantages and disadvantages to using either type.

Plastic leader may not break as easily, but it may stretch if it is put under the stress of fast stops and starts. Plastic leader is easier to work with, and is often marked at 7 1/2" intervals. It is a simple task to insert 5 seconds of silence. You just have to count off five marked intervals if your tape is running at 7.5 IPS.

The first step in the editing process is to precisely locate the section of tape to be removed. On some tape decks that can be done by manually cueing the tape. Mark the tape carefully and avoid getting ink or wax on the heads or transport mechanism of the tape player.

Next, use an editing block and a demagnetized razor blade to cut the tape at the places marked.

Warning: Editing will destroy or seriously cut any material recorded on the other side of the tape. If editing is anticipated, record on only one side of the tape.

Then, perform the following steps using splicing tape or edit tabs. (Never use cellophane tape [scotch tape], that will cause disastrous results as the adhesive will spread and contaminate the heads.)

1. Overlap the ends to be spliced by approximately 1/2 inch and align them carefully.
2. Cut through the center of the overlapped area at a 45- to 60- degree angle. Many splicing blocks will have grooves to guide this cut.
3. Butt the slanted ends of the cut tape together. Use a straightedge or ruler to assure a perfectly straight alignment.
4. Apply splicing tape to the base side of the tape (opposite to the tape side that touches the head).
5. Place the spliced connection on a hard surface and rub the splicing tape briskly with your fingernail or other hard smooth object. This is to assure a firm adherence to the splicing tape.
6. Trim off the excess splicing tape. You may cut slightly into the recording tape to insure complete removal of the excess. Edit tabs, available from Edit All, eliminate the need to cut splicing tape. The tab can be lifted from it's backing sheet, placed on the splice, and then rubbed with a fingernail. The acetate carrier can be peeled back, leaving the splice attached. This permanent splice may be stronger than the tape itself.
7. When attaching blank leader tape onto your tapes, follow the same procedures given here for splicing.

Script Analysis

Before designing sound for a play, it is important to gain knowledge about the kind of theatre it is, whether it is a traditional proscenium, laboratory theatre or studio space. You should determine when and where the play is set as that will play a large factor in the kinds of sources and sound effects you will generate. You should make notes as you read the play and see where specific sounds are indicated. You must make a decision, in conjunction with the director, on whether you will have pre-show, intermission or exit music and if the production requires atmospheric sounds. You might ask the following questions as you read the play: What information must be conveyed by sound? What sounds are important?

Later on in technical rehearsal you must sit in the auditorium and set levels for loudspeakers and mixer. Try to sample several different seats in order to hear how it will sound to the audience. You should go over the mixing console procedures and preview each sound effect and source with the board opera-tor. If there are quick cues or follow cues, you should go over the sequence prior to entering into a tech with other production elements. A "dry" technical rehearsal just for sound will help it come together quicker and more completely. Of course, if the production requires microphones, you must arrange to have a special rehearsal with the performers who will wear mics. You should make sure that the cues can be executed within the time demands of the play. Below is an excerpt from *Two Can Play* by Trevor Rhone. Read the selection through and make notes on where the cues are. Appendix G describes how to make a cue sheet for this selection.

Two Can Play

Act One Scene One

{*Incidental reggae music continues over as the house lights go to black. The actors come on in the blackness. The stage lights come up slowly, as gun shots explode in the distance and dogs bark frantically. JIM and GLORIA are lying in bed.*}

JIM: Gloria?

GLORIA: Yes, Jim

          {*Gunshots, dogs barking*}

JIM: Hear dey... is wa out dey.

{*Gunshots getting louder*}

JIM: We under seige tonight, Gloria.

GLORIA: Go to sleep, Jim.

JIM :   But Gloria–it getting closer

GLORIA: Put a pillow over yuh head.

{*Barrage of loud gunshots*}

JIM:.   It gettin' closer still... Listen...

[GLORIA *gets up off the bed and goes to the bathroom.*]

JIM: Where yuh going? ... Gloria?

[GLORIA *returns with a glass of water. She gives it to him with a pill which she takes from a pillow kept in the bed head.*]

GLORIA: Here.

Practicum

1. Record about twenty seconds of a single tone onto a tape. Then cut and splice the tape at about the 10 second mark. Play back the spliced tape, listening for any "pop" or "click" sound when tracking over the cut that indicates a poor splice.

2. Select a poem or section of a play. Design and record sound effects to go along with a narration. Some suggested material: *The Shooting of Dan McGrew* by Robert Service, or *Mrs. Murgatroyd's Dime*, a radio play. The former has cold winds, honky-tonk piano and gunshots; the latter has footsteps explosions and a talking coin that goes from sidewalk to pocket.

15 INTERCOM AND PAGING

Among the many technical elements of production, invariably the one that receives the least attention prior to the dress rehearsal is backstage communication. However, none of the scene shifts, lighting or sound cues would be able to take place were it not for the ability of the stage manager to give an audible cue. The actors would remain in the green room without hearing the command "places" or being able to hear the progress of the show through a monitor speaker. Yet such an important aspect of the theatre is often taken for granted, or left until the last minute for the sound or lighting technician to set up.

Production Communication

One of the ways in which cues were given before the advent of electricity was by means of whistles. Certain patterns of whistling would initiate a variety of scenic transformations. Among the myths of the theatre is that whistling in the playhouse is bad luck. It is easy to see how this superstition originated. Imagine the confusion that would result if a false whistle triggered a complex series of wing, border and machine action.

In order to communicate effectively in the theatre of today, prior planning must take into account the needs of creative and support personnel during rehearsals and performance. The different types of communication required during technical rehearsals are:

1. The stage manager sits in the house and communicates with the director, designers, running crew and follow spot operators to set cues.
2. The lighting designer sits in the house and communicates with the master electrician in the booth or backstage and follow spot operators up in lighting positions to set light cues.
3. The sound designer sits in the house and communicates with the sound operator to set levels for sound cues.

During the actual performance the needs are for:

1. Cues and warnings from the stage manager to the running crews, master electrician, sound operator and pin rail.
2. Acknowledgement and status reports from the crew back to the stage manager.

3. Coordination between the stage manager and house manager for curtain and intermission.
4. Cues and warnings from the stage manager to the actors.
5. Monitoring action on stage in the booths and in the dressing rooms so that the stage manager, crew and actors can hear the progress of the performance.

All of the functions listed above, except the last, may be accomplished by a well-designed intercom system. The live monitoring may be accomplished with a dedicated P.A. system. Both types of systems should be installed in a reasonably equipped theatre. These should have the capability of operating independent of the main sound reinforcement and playback system, but may be capable of interconnecting with the main system in order to hear program information.

Layout

The figure below shows a typical layout of intercom stations for a University Theatre. The location, purpose, and type of each station is as follows:

1. **Dressing rooms.** A wardrobe person or assistant stage manager working with actors will be able to keep in contact with the stage manager. Headset and/or speaker station.

2. **Upstage right.** Running Crew uses this for cueing. Headset station with belt-pack.

3. **Upstage left.** Running crew uses this for cueing. Headset station with belt-pack.

4. **Grid or load floor.** For loading weights or rigging. Headset and speaker station. When loading weights a hands-free station is needed. If a running crew member is up on the grid, as might be required to gently float leaves on cue in the final scene of *Cyrano de Bergerac*, a headset is required to minimize noise during the show.

5. **Downstage right.** Running crew or assistant stage manager uses this for cueing. Headset station.

6. **Downstage left.** Running crew or assistant stage manager uses this for cueing. Headset station.

7. **Fly rail.** Fly crew uses this for cueing. Headset station with multiple outlets.

8. **Orchestra pit.** Conductor in a musical will use this for cueing. Headset station.

9. Lighting position. Follow spot operator will use this for cueing. Headset station.

10. Lighting position. Follow spot operator will use this for cueing. Headest station.

11. House position. Stage manager and designers use this during technical rehearsal. Headset station with multiple outlets.

12. Control booth. Stage manager uses this or backstage station to call the show. Headset station.

13. Control booth. Master electrician uses this for cueing. Headset station.

14. Sound booth. Sound operator uses this for cueing. Headset station.

15. House control. House manager uses this to communicate with the stage manager. Telephone handset station.

When specifying a system for installation, the number of stations and the

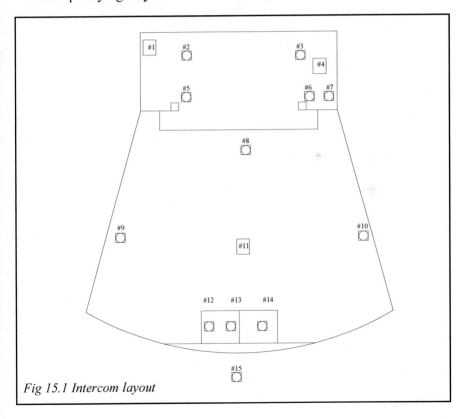

Fig 15.1 Intercom layout

number of channels must be considered. A simple system may have only two channels, A and B. In a two channel system most cues would be called on the "A" channel and cues for special effects or follow spots could be on the "B" channel. More versatile systems will have multiple channels. Four channel systems with A, B, C, and D are common.

Other choices for each station are whether it has an internal speaker, requires a belt pack or can be used with a headset directly connected to the wall station itself. The advantage in having an internal speaker is that "hands-free" operation is possible. The disadvantage is that the audience may be able to hear the cues, and that is unacceptable. Internal speakers should only be used in locations away from the audience's hearing range, like in a dressing room apart from the stage. The advantage of a belt pack is that the technician may be mobile while having control over switching, muting, and signaling other stations. The only advantage of a wall station that can be used without a belt pack is that it only requires a headset for operation. Belt packs can get misplaced easily. If the theatre is equipped with stations that will not work without a belt pack, your ability to communicate may be limited if belt packs are lost or misplaced. Both belt packs and wall stations usually have a call light to signal the operator when the headset is removed.

Clear-Com

Starting as a small garage operation inthe late 1960s, Bob Cohen and some friends were engaged in building and renting a sound reinforcement system for rock groups in San Francisco. Prior to venue, the promoter requested an intercom system to communicate with the spotlight operators. The result was beginning of the Clear-Com Intercom System.

Clear-Com was established in 1970 and is a recognized leader in the manufacture of high-quality, closed-circuit intercom systems. The system is connected via microphone cables to provide a reliable, versatile and private system. Unlike telephone systems which have a narrow bandwidth, Clear-Com's main function is to convey clear speech at all volumes and under all conditions.

Fig 15.2 Clear-Com 2-Channel Portable Main Station

Clear-Com is a distributed

amplifier system: each intercom station and beltpack contains its own mic preamplifier, power amplifier for headset and/or speaker, and signaling circuitry. The system does not rely upon a central amplifier. The method of connecting an audio line to an input is via bridging with high impedance, keeping audio levels constant, even when stations join or leave the line. A

Fig 15.3 Clear-Com RS-502 Beltpack

Clear-Com station's input impedance is about 100 times the impedance of the line connected to that station, so it draws very little audio power. A Main Station or Power Supply provides the DC power (30 volts) and the line termination (200 ohms) for the system. Line levels never drop, even if intercoms join or leave a system. If one station stops working, the rest of the system continues operating normally. All stations are compatible.

The "call" function lets a station operator attract the attention of other operators who have removed their headsets or turned off their speakers. Pressing a station's call button turns on the lamps at stations on the same channel. "Call" also activates remote paging. The remote paging function lets remote stations be designated for announcement via their built-in speakers.

Sidetone adjustment allows the operator to set their own voice level as heard in the headset/speaker system. Sidetone adjustment never affects incoming or outgoing signals.

Paging

Although paging of dressing rooms and other areas may be done through a production intercom system with a combination of headset and built-in speakers, a better solution is to install a separate system dedicated exclusively for that purpose. A 70-volt system is ideal for this purpose (see Chapter 4). In such a system speakers can be switched in and out with no deterioration of the signal. The stage manager may then page the dressing rooms without breaking the attention of the production crew. Pre-show house announcements concerning cast changes or photograph policy can be made through speakers mounted permanently in the house without interfering with the main production speaker system. Finally, the action on stage may be monitored and sent to the dressing rooms, production booths or lobby for latecomers to hear until they can be seated.

A permanent paging system may also be used for a lecture or symposium. It is relatively easy to plug microphones into a permanent system, turn on mixer, amp and speakers, set levels, and satisfy the requirements of lecturer, panelists and audience. The Shure M267 is a compact four channel mixer designed for professional applications. It features four switchable microphone or line-level balanced inputs with individual gain controls and low-frequency rolloff switches. The output is switchable for line and microphone level or as an additional unbalanced line feed to drive a tape recorder or power amplifier. It also has simplex power (phantom power) for condenser microphones. A front-panel headphone level control and monitor jack is available for headphones. The unit may be stacked with others to increase the number of channels. Placed in a rack together with an amplifier that has a 70-volt output and an array of permanently mounted speakers, a system can be assembled that will satisfy most of the the paging and monitoring needs in a theatre.

It must be emphasized that a key aspect of such a system is the permanently wired speaker array. A constant-voltage, line-matching transformer designed to match the speaker with a 70-volt line must be used for each speaker. A number of speakers mounted in the wall and ceiling of production areas, green room, dressing rooms and audience, offer an efficient and flexible solution to paging requirements.

16 WEB AUDIO

Whether delivering audio over the Internet is feasible for theatre applications remains to be seen, but the technology is advancing so rapidly that there is a good chance that delivery of sound effects on the Web is not as far fetched as some would imagine. It is easy to find many audio "clips" online and basically there are three choices for delivering audio over the Internet: 1.) you can select an audio file and play it immediately using a player on your computer; 2.) you can download the audio file and save it for listening later using your own player or 3.) you can use an "audio streaming" technology such as RealAudio™ Assuming that you have the right hardware, such as a Pentium PC with a sound card, software to convert audio formats and plenty of disk space, you can do some amazing things with web sound. The importance of large capacity disks cannot be understated. A popular audio format is the WAV file and a ten minute selection recorded in 16-bit stereo at 44kHz requires over 120 MB. You'll probably need a hard drive of at least 4 Gigabytes to do any meaningful sound recording and editing.

The first thing you must to is to select your source, whether it is a microphone or line-level device such as a CD player or tape deck. You should make sure that your sound card has both mic and line inputs so that you have the option. You can often record right off the CD player in your PC. The software that comes bundled with your sound card will let you select the source, input level and file names for the digital recording. Rules for signal-to-noise ratios apply here as well. Make sure that if you are using a live mic that it is placed away from the computer so that you don't pick up fan noise, key clicks or hard drive sounds. Make sure you have the highest input level possible without distortion. The sound software program will have a visual representation of a fader for your sources. You set the input levels by selecting the fader with your mouse and then sliding it to the desired level. It is best to make a test recording and play it back before your final attempt. The actual recording is very simple, you play your source and hit a "record" icon on your screen. When finished, you click on "stop."

After recording, you can edit your audio file with unprecedented ease. If you have used leader and splicing tape before, you won't believe the simplicity of editing the actual waveform of your sound bytes. You can select a section of the sound and cut, paste or copy it. It works just like a word processor for sound. There are also some effects built into some software editing programs such as reverb, EQ, noise filters and gates. Of course, you could also use your conventional signal processing equipment prior to recording it with the computer.

When you are done, the final step is to save your file. The WAV file is the most common, but if you are doing broadcast sound you may want to use the RA format (Real Audio), which requires a special encorder. Web sound has not made inroads into live theatre performance, but RealAudio (and RealVideo) offer the potential for simultaneous broadcasting of your program material over the Internet. You may need to consult with your systems administrator to set up your server to handle live broadcasting, but you don't need to do anything like that to receive the broadcasts other than install the requisite software on your equipped PC.

If you would like to add sound to your website or edit digital sound effects for your production, you'll want to explore a software product such as ProTools or Sonic Foundry's new suite of audio tools. Sonic Foundry offers two software programs with over 800 free music tracks and sound effects. You can record and edit your audio files with a superb PC audio editing program, Sound Forge XP 4.5. Then you can combine, overlay and create multiple track recordings with the second program - Acid Style. The software is extremely easy to use. It features the familiar Windows toolbars and simple click-and-drag commands. When you start Sound Forge XP, you will see the main screen where you do your editing. You can open an existing sound file or record a new one. Each time you open a sound file it has its own window. When you open a window, the Process, Effects and Tools menus are listed which provide editing functions. The status bar displays help, playback sample rate, sample size, mono/stereo and total length of the active data window and total free storage space. There are two main toolbars, the Standard toolbar provides access to the common functions, the Transport toolbar contains the Record, Play, Rewind and other control buttons. As you would expect in the Windows interface, you can move the toolbars anywhere on the screen. The data window displays the waveform along with a time ruler, level indicator, status and controls. Once you open a file you can play it by selecting the Play button on the Transport toolbar. While the file is playing, a pointer will move along the waveform showing the current position. You can play from any point by simply moving the cursor. Move your cursor, left-click. You can also play portions of the wave by clicking and dragging. There is a playbar in the data window which may be used instead of the transport tools. You can magnify or zoom to view portions of the file. The cut, copy and paste functions are active as well. You can trim and crop a section of data to customize your effect. Then you can mix by combining two sounds together into one window so you can create complex sound effects.

Sound Forge's Acid Style software makes it easy to make loop based music. You can select pre-recorded sound clips and combine them as you wish on a maximum of eight tracks. If that is not enough, you can upgrade to Acid Music, which allows you to add an unlimited number of tracks. Acid Style consists of a library of pre-recorded loops and an editing screen that allows you to select and manipulate the loops, assembling them into a piece of music and then save and playback the results. There are two ways to add loops to the Track List, you can double click or drag and drop. Once you've established your loops in the track list, you then create events on each track. An event is a loop that you place on a track programmed to repeat at a specific time at a specified volume. The track view will show the waves inside of color rectangles. The length of the rectangle indicates the duration of the event. You use the Pencil tool to click in the track, then hold the mouse and drag the cursor, placing the loop on the track. You can use the Erase tool to remove sections of the track. Then press the Play button to listen to it. Then you can use the individual controls for that track, including level and pan. You've got a fader and two arrow buttons. You will be amazed at how easy it is to create music and sound effects. You can sample sound effects from commercial CDs, such as the BBC Sound Effects Library, and use them to compose multi-layered sound cues. If you want to change the tempo of the project, move the Tempo slider in the lower left corner of the Track View. This can even be done in real time as the project is playing. There is time compression and expansion being done on all of the loops to match the project tempo. While the algorithm is very good, there are still some limitations. You probably will not be able to get a 120 bpm loop to sound great at 60 bpm.

MP3

MP3 is the latest digital audio compression format that has become a popular standard for listening to music on the web. MP3, technically named MPEG, compresses audio data and encodes it into a frame-based format. The file is decoded in playback. Since an MP3 file coded in this way may contain information shared between frames, it is not easy to edit. There is a way to do it if your audio editing software supports MP3 import, decoding and saving in an uncompressed audio file format, but there is noticeable degradation. You would have to decode it to an uncompressed file, then edit and save, but the result is a copy that is of lower quality than the original MP3 sound file.

MP3 has also caused concern among recording industry executives and artists such as Metallica who have taken companies to court for copyright infringement. They want to unplug the music distribution services run by My.MP3.com and Napster. Metallica made a list of 335,000 fans who are illegally downloading its music using Napster and asked the company to ban the practice.

The original MP3.com strategy was to offer free songs by independent artists. This created a cottage industry with garage bands self-producing their own music in MP3 format. Users can download an MP3 player such as Winamp and save songs on their hard drives or copy them to a CD. Things became complicated when Napster and MP3.com created software programs that let Internet users find and share songs. You place your favorite music CD in your computer's CD drive and MP3s "Beam-it" software verifies that it is authentic, then converts the files to MP3 format. Users can listen to the songs in streaming MP3 format on any computer, but can't download the file.

Napster works in a similar fashion. A user records and stores MP3 formatted songs in a folder on his or her hard drive. Then a central directory keeps track of which users are logged on, cataloging the songs in each user's special folder. A user searches throught the Napster directory for a desired song and downloads it from any computer on the system that has the song. New services such as Gnutella lets users share files with each other directly without going through a central computer. At the request of the user, the files are available for others to "unlock" streaming versions of the songs and play. Once the song is downloaded it can be played with any MPs decoder, including Winamp, Real Jukebox or Windows Media player.

The music file can also be sent to another person as an e-mail attachment or stored on a portable player like the Rio. More than a million MP3 files are available on Napster, many of them pirated from commercial CDs. Indiana University and Yale have shut down access to the service not only because it is such a hit among college students that it has jammed their computer networks, but also because of the legal implications. The 1998 Digital Millenium

Copyright Act (DMCA) is designed to protect artists from online pirates. However, there is a provision that protects Internet service providers from liability if subscribers download illegal files without their knowledge. The Recording Industry of America along with many music compaines filed suit against MP3.com and Napster. In 2001, the United States District Court sided with the record companies; Napster must refrain from making copyrighted songs available for downloading.

Future Directions

The digital delivery of music is small in comparison with traditional music sales. Digital music sales are expected to be around $150 million by 2003 which is dwarfed by the $14 billion in music sales in 1999. However, MP3 has created a frenzy for Internet music by making online distribution of high-quality recordings possible. MP3 is forcing the development of new models which will benefit artists with a royalty system, but currently there is a conflict between the old strictly-controlled distribution modes and the freewheeling distribution channels of the Internet. in 1999 the RIAA created the Secure Digital Music Initiative to control the playback of an audio file. The key is to package secure audio in a playable package. Look for the big record companies to adopt the technique and move large libraries of music online available by subscription, perhaps even "per play" like an old jukebox in the future.

Audiences accustomed to "surround sound" installations at home come to a show with high expectations for live sound reproduction. MIDI, SMPTE and other timecode schemes allow the linkage of light control and sound with other MIDI devices, so that music could initiate light cues or motion sensors could trigger sound and light effects. This is not as far-fetched as it seems since we have done such things on stage for at least ten years. However, the miniaturization of circuits has resulted in the design of sound cards containing all the signal processing functions you can imagine. In the past, we'd have an assortment of components for reverb, delay, pitch change, flanging, gating, EQ and noise reduction. Then we saw the development of the "digital effects processor," which was a box containing stock effects with changeable parameters (e.g. you could adjust the time of a delay or the frequency of a pitch change). Now and in the future, all of these can be housed on a PC card with a DSP chip (digital signal processing).

Look for the development of "smart" components, such as loudspeakers, microphones, mixers and amplifiers. This trend has already begun with auto-mated faders and memory for mixing consoles, but imagine if you had a smart microphone that could automatically EQ a performer's voice or intelligent wireless systems that monitor the signal and filter out annoying buzzes, pops and clicks that are still too common on our stages. How about an amplifier that has a self-diagnosis chip to determine impedance overloads or component failure?

Keyboards are everywhere in the theatre and many are compatible with your computer and lightboard via a MIDI connection. Pre-packaged sounds, drums and special effects are common features of the new generation of keyboards. Many have built in "samplers" for recording sound effects. DAT (digital audio tape), CD-Audio and MiniDisk technologies enable the recording of extremely high quality, low noise sound effects and music. Instruments and recording devices will work together with computer software products such as Cakewalk, one of the first and best programs for multitrack digital audio recording and/or MIDI sequencing. The latest Pro-Audio software will let you record 24 simultaneous tracks with reverb, flange, chorus EQ, delay echo, time compression and expansion as well as pitch shifting. Look also for higher sampling rates as the cost of memory continues to drop. The computer is in the sound booth and studio from now on and we expect to hear the difference in our theatres.

Theatre is a collaborative art and technology has enabled designers, directors and producers to share images and text in unprecedented ways via the Internet and World Wide Web. E-mail has replaced letter writing as a quick, direct mode of communication. You can attach a sound or video file to your electronic messages. Presently most of us connect to the Internet through relatively slow telephone modem connections. New technologies such as cable modems, ISDN and the super-fast DSL (Digital Subscriber Line) will be about five times faster and permit simultaneous voice transmission. Think of the possibilities for inter-regional and international collaborations, or just having a production meeting with a designer who happens to be momentarily out of town on another project. Fast internet connections in the future will permit rapid file transfers of images, designs and schedules. The web has changed the way we interact with each other and it is in the process of revolutionizing the way our computers work. The files on your computer will all be "web" compatible in the future. The operating system that controls your computer operations will also be a browser once the government and Microsoft work out their anti-trust agreement. The old paradigm of the past held that data would be stored in centralized "mainframes" with enormous databases. The way the computer future is shaping up, it appears that "distributed computing" will be the paradigm for the 21st century. Our local PCs will be connected and linked to all of the other local PCs in the world and file sharing will be routine. Total network connectivity will spawn new procedures for software companies. You will be able to authorize they're entrance into your system over the Internet and give you software upgrades and enhancements while you are sleeping. Lighting and sound companies can come through the network, access your hard drive, get customer and user data, upgrade the software, send you an e-mail that it's done. The designer might take advantage of this feature by updating sketches sent out to shops without leaving the studio.

There are also new experiments in the creation of virtual theatre over the Internet, such as the ATHE MOOS (Association for Theatre in Higher Education - Multiple Object – Oriented game). These are theatre environments based upon the old adventure game format (i.e. you are in a virtual world and encounter others, making decisions about properties and behaviors).

Other possibilities are that you could save designs to a website and access archives of images and designs to integrate into your projects. We are already able to view most of the famous paintings in the world on our computers over the World Wide Web. Technology will undoubtedly outpace copyright law in this regard.

WIRE AND CONNECTORS

One of the most critical and certainly the most vulnerable parts of the sound hookup are the lengths of cable and the connectors. Among the problems that may occur are internal wire breakage, faulty connectors and cold solder connections. A few guidelines:

1. Do not wrap the cables around your elbow. A figure eight loop is best.
2. Do not disconnect cables by pulling connectors.
3. Check for continuity periodically using a VOM or cable tester especially designed for that purpose. (see Inputs and Outputs).

When selecting cable, consider the distance, the gauge, and the amount of wear the cable will take. The length of cable for a given wire size can be doubled if twice the power loss can be tolerated. The next smaller gauge can be used if twice the power loss can be tolerated and the length remains the same.

The chart below may be used for constant voltage systems.

The choice of appropriate audio cables for runs of varying distances depends on many factors, such as amplifier voltage output and power level as

Wire size (AWG)	Low impedance 10% power loss						High impedance 5% power loss					
	4 Ohm		8 Ohm		16 Ohm		100 Ohm		250 Ohm		500 Ohm	
	ft	m	ft	m	ft	m	ft	m	ft	m	ft	m
14	88	27	176	54	352	101	1045	319	2610	796	5220	159
16	55	17	110	34	220	67	630	192	1574	430	3150	96
18	35	11	70	21	140	43	410	235	1020	311	2050	82
20	22	7	44	13	88	27	262	80	655	200	1310	39
22	13	4	26	8	52	16	164	49	410	125	820	25
24	8	2	16	5	32	10	105	32	262	80	525	16

well as load impedance and the percent of power loss which can be tolerated. For this reason it is not practical to provide a general chart showing the recommended wire size for all conditions. The chart shows the maximum recommended cable runs for various wire sizes selected for commonly encountered load impedances.

The XLR Connector

Signal connections in professional audio installations are best made with XLR-type connections. The microphone input (female), line input (female) and line output (male) must be wired properly to the mating plugs. Refer to Figure 35 and follow the procedures below.

For balanced inputs, wire the XLR connector as follows:
1. Connect the signal leads of a two-conductor shielded cable to pin 2 (high) and pin 3 (low) of the connector.
2. Connect the cable shield to pin 1.

For unbalanced inputs using two-conductor shielded cable, wire the male XLR connector as follows:
1. Connect the signal leads of a cable to pin 2 (high) and pin 3 (low) of the connector.
2. Connect the cable shield to pin 1 of the connector.
3. Connect a jumper from pin 1 to pin 2 of the connector.

For unbalanced inputs using single-conductor shielded cable, wire the male XLR as follows:
1. Connect the center conductor of the single-conductor shielded cable to pin 3 of the connector.
2. Connect the cable shield to pins 1 and 2.

Neutrik Speakon Connector

Neutrik makes a wide variety of XLR, 1/4" DIN and phono connectors, jacks, patch cables and accessories. One of their most outstanding products that is rapidly becoming an industry standard is the 2-pole Speakon connector, an excellent choice for loudspeaker panels and cable connectors. It features a quick locking system with options for soldered or screw-type solderless connections for easy repair in the the field. The Speakon is recommended over 1/4" or two-pole twist lock connectors for loudspeakers.

The MIDI Connector

The MIDI cable is a standard 5-pin DIN connector. As shown in the diagram below pin #4 is designated for the signal plus and pin #5 carries the signal minus. Pin #2, at the center of the 5-pin configuration, is used for ground-to-shield, Pins #1 and #3 are not required in the MIDI specification, but may be used for sync pulses. When MIDI devices are connected, "out" plugs into "in" and "in" plugs into "out." A thru jack transmits information identical to whatever arrived at the in jack. "Thru" plugs into "in." A MIDI cable carries data in only one direction.

MIDI is not a piece of hardware. It is a communications protocol agreed upon by the MIDI Manufacturers Association (MMA) and the Japan MIDI Standards Committee (JMSC). MIDI data is digital. Information is provided to a receiving device that understands MIDI. It is not an audio signal in the sense that the MIDI signal itself is audible. The sound initiated by a MIDI event depends entirely upon how the receiving device interprets the MIDI command. The MIDI specifications are applied by each manufacturer in different ways. Although basic connections for MIDI devices are the same, different functions may be controlled by the same channel. A manufacturer who abides by the specifications only agrees not to send anything out of the MIDI output jack that does not conform to the protocol.

Ground-
to-Shield

Signal
Minus (-)

Signal
Plus (+)

#2

#5

#4

#3

#1

May be used for Sync
Pulse with Drum Machine

MIDI connector wiring.

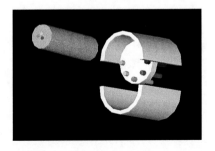

Strain relief fitting
Shell
Insulating collar
Female insert

Cable clamp & screws
Set screw
Locking tab

WIRING A FEMALE XLR CONNECTOR

Parts identification (as the connector is usually packaged).

Insert strain relief in rear of shell. Then slip shell onto cable end, followed by insulating collar. Strip outer insulation approximately 9/16". (No. 8451 cable illustrated here)

Pull off foil wrap. Strip approximately 5/16" of insulation from the center conductors, leaving approximately 1/4" of insulation between the bare wire and the outer insulation. Tin the center conductors, and trim so that about 1/8" bare wire remains. Then tin the shield conductor, orienting it with the center conductors so they are aligned with the proper pins of the insert. Cut the end of the shield so that it extends 1/16" beyond the center conductors.

Solder the center conductors to their respective pins, using just enough solder to fill the end of the pin. Yamaha's wiring standard dictates that the black lead mates with pin 3, the white (or red) lead with 2 (see footnote on page 10 of this section). Then solder the shield to pin 1. Clean off any solder splashes, and inspect for burned insulation. Insert the locking tab in the female insert, as illustrated, with small nib facing front of connector.

Slide insulating collar foward, up to rear edge of female insert. The outer insulation of the cable must be flush with, or covered by the end of the insert. If any of the center conductors are visible, the cable clamp may not be able to grip the cable firmly, and the connector leads will soon fatigue. Then slide the collar back into the shell.

Slide the shell forward, orienting the notch in the shell with the locking tab in the insert. Secure the insert in the shell with the set screw. Place the cable clamp over the rear of the shell, with careful attention to the clamp's orientation; a raised lip inside the clamp should be aligned immediately over a lip in the shell for thinner cables (No. 8451). For heavier cables (No. 8412), the clamp should be turned around to offset the lips and provide more clearance for the cable. Insert the clamp screws and tighten fully.

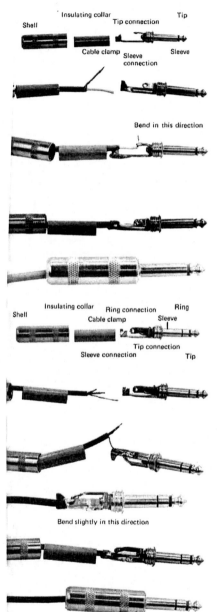

WIRING A STANDARD PHONE PLUG (2-conductor)

Parts identification.

Slide shell, then insulating collar over cable end. Strip outer insulation for length equal to length of sleeve connection. Unwrap or unbraid shield, twist to form lead.

Position outer insulation just ahead of cable clamp, strip center conductor from point just behind tip connection. Tin center conductor and shield. Bend shield as illustrated, solder to outer surface of sleeve connection. (Cool immediately with pliers.) Insert center conductor in tip connection, solder, cut end flush. Bend the end of the tip connector (slightly) toward the sleeve connection to help prevent the burr (from the cut wire) from cutting through the insulating collar.

Using pliers, bend cable clamp around outer insulation. Clamp should be firm, but not so tight as to cut insulation.

Slide insulating collar forward, until flush with rear of threads. Slide shell forward, screw tight to plug assembly.

WIRING A TIP, RING & SLEEVE PHONE PLUG (3-conductor)

Parts identification.

Slide shell and insulating collar over cable end. Strip outer insulation for length equal to length of sleeve connection. Remove any tracer cords and strain relief cords. Form lead from shield. Hold cable with outer insulation just ahead of cable clamp, and strip the red (or white) conductor just behind the tip connection. Then strip the black conductor just behind the ring connection. Tin all leads, and cut the center conductors so approximately 1/8" of bare wire remains.

Solder the shield to the outer surface of the sleeve connection, allowing enough free shield to bend around to the other side of the cable clamp. Cool the connection immediately with pliers.

Insert the center conductor leads in their respective connection points, and solder in place. Trim the leads flush. Bend the end of the tip connection (slightly) toward the ring connection to help prevent the burr (from the cut wire) from cutting through the insulating collar.

Using pliers, bend the cable clamp around the outer insulation. The clamp should be firm, but not so tight as to cut the insulation.

Slide the insulating collar forward, until flush with rear of threads. Slide the shell forward, and screw tightly onto plug.

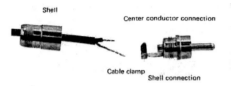

Shell
Center conductor connection
Cable clamp
Shell connection

WIRING AN RCA-TYPE PIN PLUG*

Parts identification and cable preparation.

Strip approximately 1/2" of outer insulation. Unwrap or unbraid the shield and form a lead. Strip approximately 5/16" of insulation from the center conductor. Tin both leads.

Solder the shield to the outer surface of the shell connection, allowing enough free shield to wrap the cable around to the center of the connector. Cool the connection immediately with pliers.

Insert the center conductor in the hollow pin, and fill that end with solder. Cool the connection immediately with pliers. Clean any solder splashes and inspect for burned insulation. Pinch the clamp around the outer insulation with pliers, firmly, but not so tight as to cut the insulation.

Slide the shell forward and screw it tightly to the threaded plug.

*Switchcraft No. 3502 connector illustrated. Many large diameter cables are more easily wired to "simple" RCA type pin plugs without a shell (Switchcraft No. 3501M, or equivalent). The braid can then be soldered directly to the shell of the plug.

B TURNTABLES AND CARTRIDGES

Description

The turntable was one of the most basic components in an audio system but has now been largely relegated to the dustbin of audio history except for major use in dance clubs. There seems to be a resurgence of vinyl fever in some cities such as London and New York with oldies and new pressings on display. Some audiophiles still insist that the best turntable and cartridge performs at a level superior to digital. Turntables merited an entire chapter in the first edition of this book. Today, the spinning disk and scratching needle remain important enough to be included in this appendix.

A turntable must rotate at a selected speed with no fluctuations, and provide a vibration-free environment for the record. The first sound reproducing devices made by Thomas Edison were hand-cranked cylinders, later replaced by spring-wound phonographs. Most turntables today are driven by electric motors. Electrically driven machines are very accurate devices, with less than 1% deviation in designated speed. The method by which the power from the motor is transferred to the turntable platter classifies the drive mechanism. The three most common types are belt-drive, rim- or idler-driven and direct-drive.

A belt-drive turntable has a single motor connected to the platter by means of a belt. Speed, measured in revolutions per minute (rpm), is varied by shifting the belt from one pulley to another. In the basic belt drive system, a lever moves the belt across a stepped pulley to change between 45 and 33 1/3 rpm. The disadvantage of the belt drive system is that the belt may slip or deteriorate.

A rim-drive turntable uses a combination of idler wheel and motor to transfer the power to the rim of the platter. This system is not known for high performance and was commonly found on cheap portable phonographs that were used in schools for classes. Many

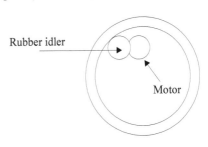

Rubber idler

Motor

Direct drive mechanism

machines designed for children employed the idler, or puck method.

In a direct-drive turntable the motor drives the shaft directly. The motor, and thus the speed, may be quartz-controlled. This has several advantages. Direct-drive turntables can start fast without hesitation and pitch may be changed by varying the speed. Although direct-drive turntables are quite common, belt-drive units are preferred for demanding applications due to their ability to eliminate low-frequency rumble. However, if you dub records on to tape for dance, you may want the speed variation capability of a direct-drive turntable for precise rhythmic accompaniment.

The tonearm is another component of a turntable system that must be considered. There are two main types, pivoted and tangential. The pivoted tonearm is the most common one, where the tonearm is attached on one side of the platter and pivots to move across the record. The tangential tracking method moves the stylus across the record in a linear fashion. Although this seems to be quite modern, it was actually used by Edison who used a feed screw to track the needle across his original cylinder.

The tonearm must track the groove across the record while supporting the cartridge and stylus at a specific height. Built-in antiskating devices and adjustable counterweights will accommodate different cartridge weights and tracking forces to minimize the friction between stylus and record groove.

As you are well aware, the trend now is towards compact disc or digital recordings. However, before scrapping the turntable, remember that many old jazz and classical recordings will never be available on CD. Those old albums and sound effects records are valuable. Keep the turntable, and you can improve its sound simply by obtaining a better cartridge. The best turntables and cartridge assemblies still rival some digital reproduction methods.

The phono cartridge is one of the smallest and, in many ways, the least understood of audio components. Despite its diminutive size, the cartridge performs a seemingly impossible task. When picking up the two channels of a stereo program, the stylus is simultaneously deflected laterally and vertically at frequencies that can exceed 15 kHz,

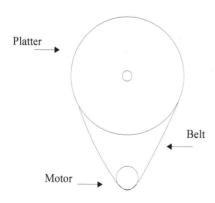

Platter

Belt

Motor

Belt drive mechanism

sometimes experiencing accelerations in excess of 30 times the acceleration of gravity. Despite these severe conditions, the stylus must remain in continual contact with the groove walls or blatant distortion will result.

The part of the cartridge that converts the vibrations of the stylus into an output voltage is called the transducer. Many types of transducer systems are available today, each with its own theoretical advantages and disadvantages. Yet designers have discovered ingenious ways to circumvent the problems inherent in each type, and many of them are capable of excellent performance. Regardless of the type of transducer, all high quality cartridges are engineered with the same performance goals in mind: (1) ability to keep the stylus in contact with the groove walls at all times; (2) flat frequency response over the entire audible frequency range; (3) inaudible distortion; (4) a high degree of channel separation; and, (5) output voltage and impedance to match the input characteristics of preamps.

Two basic transducer types are used to generate a pickup's output voltage: magnetic and nonmagnetic. Magnetic transducers, which dominate the market, depend for their operation on changing the magnetic flux that cuts through a wire, generally one that has been formed into a coil. In the other classes are piezolelectric (ceramic), semiconductor, and electret cartridges, none of which use magnets. The magnetic types are as follows:

Moving Magnet
Also called a fixed coil, moving magnet is the most prevalent type of cartridge. A powerful magnet is fixed to the stylus that vibrates and generates current through adjacent coils. Voltages are induced in both coils of opposite polarity.

By connecting them in the proper manner, it is possible to obtain an output voltage twice that of a single coil. Typically this is between 2mv and10 mv, a level most preamplifiers are designed to accept. Using two coils greatly reduces hum and noise. These are often called hum-bucking pickups. It is relatively easy to manufacture and replace worn or damaged styli. A prime example of the moving magnet cartridge is the Shure V15. Pickering, Ortofon, Stanton, Audio Technica, ADC, and Denon all make reasonably priced versions, usually

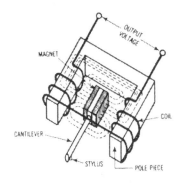

Moving magnet cartridge

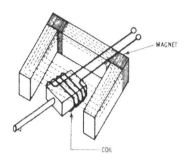

Moving coil cartridge

around $100, although there are high-end cartridges out there costing more than $1000.

Moving Coil

The operation is similar to the moving magnet, except that the coil is attached to the cantilever and the magnet is stationary. The coil must be as light as possible so that it does not impose an excessive mechanical load on the stylus cantilever (and on the record groove). The output voltage is very small, necessitating delivery to a normal phono input. It is capable of excellent performance often described as spacious with low distortion, but it is often delicate and quirky.

Since the manufacture requires considerable handiwork, it is moderately expensive. It must be returned to the factory for stylus replacement. Few are available for less than $100. An example of this type of cartridge is the Ortofon Signet MK120HE. It has a diamond stylus, a samarium-cobalt magnet and oxygen-free copper wire.

Moving Iron

Also called variable reluctance. The moving iron cartridge has a fixed magnet and coil. A small piece of iron is bonded to the end of the stylus cantilever and is the part that moves. A gap in the path (air) adds reluctance (similar to resistance, but for magnetic fields) and reduces the amount of flux. The iron

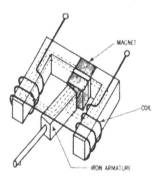

moves in the gap controlling the flux that passes from the permanent magnet to the coils, which are normally connected in a hum-bucking arrangement like that used in the moving magnet cartridge. These are relatively inexpensive to build. It has a large output voltage (large magnet, coil with many turns of wire). The stylus is replaceable by the user.

Ribbon Cartridge

The ribbon cartridge is similar to the moving coil type. An extremely light, thin piece of metallic

Moving iron cartridge

foil is attached to the cantilever. The wires form a coil with one loop. It has an output voltage similar to that of a moving coil design. The ribbon cartridge requires a pre-amp and is expensive to manufacture.

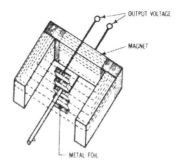

Ribbon cartridge

C TROUBLESHOOTING

A few years ago, I had the pleasure of seeing Al Pacino in Hughie by Eugene O'Neill at the Circle in the Square in New York. The sound design by John Gromada was excellent, especially the evocative atmospheric effects and wireless microphone technique used to amplify Paul Benedict's ethereal Night Clerk thoughts. Unfortunately, this wonderful theatre piece was marred by an audible hum in the loudspeaker right in front of our seats. Undoubtedly, most of the audience would not have noticed the buzzing since everyone was enthralled by the riveting acting of a true star. However, I sat in the fourth row and heard it clearly despite an otherwise flawless production.

Recently it was reported that Beverly Sills, opera diva and chairwoman of Lincoln Center, was displeased after attending a performance of the City Opera's *Il Viaggio a Reins*. She heard "a buzz, a sound in the air which makes me know something is there." The system has over two dozen microphones around the stage and orchestra and more than 100 speakers in the 2,700-seat theatre.

The persistent buzzing noise is often characteristic of electromagnetic and/ or electrostatic interference. The troublesome frequency is often referred to as "60-cycle hum," but A/C power cables are only one possible cause of loudspeaker hum. The problem is often inherent in the sound reinforcement and playback system, perhaps in the routing of speaker lines or the grounding of equipment.

The simplest way to trace any problem is to start at the amplifier and work back to the mixer. It also helps to have a headset to check the signal in the other direction beginning at the source, then the mixer, and so on until you can determine where the signal is being hurt. Above all, don't panic. Try to develop a systematic approach to troubleshooting. It may be something obvious, like a component coming unplugged or a patching problem. If you start simply and analyze your signal path carefully, you will at least be able to identify the problem.

Hum: The sound of 60-cycle current and its harmonics (120 Hz, 240 Hz, etc.) produces hum, which can be introduced into the signal path. Check all of the connections, jiggling the cable ends to detect changes in tone. If the hum stops or changes frequency, you have isolated the problem. If it is a molded plug, cut it off and replace it with a new connector. A nonmolded plug can be re-soldered. RCA plugs can be fixed by pressing the outer ground "petals" inward. Cables can also introduce hum. Check to make sure that all cables are grounded and routed away from all AC lines. Keep power cables as short as possible. Avoid coiling power cable near components as it may create an "electron field." Do not stack pre-amps on or near power amps as the transformers in the power amplifiers may induce hum into a pre-amp's circuits. If all else fails, equalization may be able to eliminate some frequencies, but remember that the signal will contain some desirable frequencies that may be cut or rolled off by EQ. If the hum is inherent in the component itself, like a noisy mixer or piece of signal processing gear, have a qualified technician analyze the circuits. An intermittent filter capacitor or failing transistor may be part of the problem.

Feedback: The sudden shriek that occurs when a singer points the microphone into the loudspeaker is an annoying and embarrassing experience for the sound engineer. Proper placement of main and monitor speakers may reduce the potential for feedback. Always do a sound check to determine how much "headroom" you have on each potentiometer. Mark these levels carefully. Know when you will approach feedback levels. Finally, power up gradually and check the microphones one at a time to have control. You will then be able to react quickly with the correct response if you hear a sudden squeal.

Pops: Turning the mixer on after the amps have been powered up will produce a nasty "pop" in the audio system. Another cause is the vocalist that gets too close to the microphone. The combination of plosive "p" and the proximity effect of increased bass may cause a potentially disastrous problem for the loudspeakers. Use windscreens or acoustic filters on the microphones. Turn on the mixer before the power amps and turn off the power amps before shutting down the mixer.

Crackles and buzzes: Pushing loudspeakers into distortion with too much signal or dirty potentiometers creates a static that irritates the senses and may destroy the speaker. Use a cleaner for potentiometer contacts. Avoid transients that may overdrive the speakers. Look for bad contacts between connectors.

RF interference: Radio frequencies may be induced from lighting dimmers, nearby transmitter towers or AC noise. Use heavy duty shielded cable. Check all ground connections and isolate dimmer and lighting cables from audio lines. Avoid ground loops.

A cable tester is an invaluable piece of test equipment to keep on hand. It is relatively easy to build one, but there are products available that are ideal for that purpose. The Whirlwind Tester is a comprehensive cable testing device that is compact and comes with belt clip for convenience. On the tester there are 5–LEDs, 2–XLR jacks, 2–1/4" jacks, 2–RCA (phono) jacks and one power switch. To test cables, it is only necessary to connect both ends of the cable according to the routing diagrams. The LEDs will light to indicate polarity and continuity. When one or more of the LEDs fail to light, the cable may be considered bad.

When testing XLR cables, all three green LEDs will light when the cable is good. If the pins 2 and 3 are reversed on an XLR connector, the red LED labeled PHASE REVERSE will light. If there is an open ground (pin 1), no LEDs will light. Readings for 1/4" cables are much the same. When using mono cables, the LED labeled PIN 2/RING will not light, since it corresponds to the ring on a stereo plug. RCA cables are tested using the 2 LEDs marked PHONO, with the top LED corresponding to ground and the bottom corresponding to hot. The device also has provisions for testing special adapter cables.

Whirlwind's Qbox is an audio line tester that includes a microphone, a speaker, a test tone generator, outputs for standard headphones, a 1/4" jack for line in or a 2kOhm (telephone) earpiece out, and voltage presence LED's for confirming phantom or intercom power.

Proper connection, grounding, high signal-to-noise ratios and periodic maintenance to clean pots and demagnetize heads may solve most of your noise problems. A lot of old graphic equalizers may add more noise, instead of improving the sound. Switch the EQ out of the system if you are not using it. When dubbing, patch the tape recorders directly together instead of running them through a mixer. Use dbx or other noise reduction whenever possible. A noise gate may also help eliminate what little noise is left. And then you can sit back and enjoy your sound emerging from total silence.

A bridging amplifier with a

Whirlwind 'Qbox' audio line tester

headset can be an invaluable tool in signal path troubleshooting. Make sure it has multiple outlets, so that you can check XLR and ¼" phone jack circuits. In recording, begin with your source checking the patch into the mixer, then through the mixer to your outputs. In a loudspeaker configuration, work from the amplifiers back through to the source making sure that the amps are properly loaded with loudspeakers.

Earth Loops and Shielding

When unbalanced equipment is connected, the screen of the cable which is carrying the signal links the cases of the mixer and amplifier. Both cases may be connected to earth for safety creating a continuous, circular path from the earth at one mains plug, through the mains cable to the mixer, through the mixer chassis to the screen of the link cable to the amplifier chassis, and back to earth via the amplifier mains cable. Then, this earth current combines with the signal in the cable giving hum in the background of the signal. The earth loop can be broken by disconnecting the earth wire in all but one of the mains plugs. This can be dangerous but may be justifiable in a permanent installation where the equipment is earthed by the screened cables

Buzzes, Pops and Clicks

Microphone cables are particularly susceptible to all forms of electrical interference. It is important that these cables be kept clear of all power cables, such as those used for lighting instruments. It may appear convenient to wrap loudspeaker or mic cable along with lighting cable to "trim" the offstage areas, but this can be deadly to a sound system. It might cause the sound system to modulate those electrostatic and electromagnetic induced currents. If your speakers "vroom" when the lights are dimmed, you had better start looking for AC cables that are in close proximity to your sound cables.

Another problem comes when "hot-patching" amplifiers and speakers. This should be avoided at all costs. If you must re-patch, turn the amp off first. Otherwise, you run the risk of causing your ears a great deal of harm, and blowing up the amp in the meantime. Never unplug a speaker while it is being driven by an amp as the amplifier may self-destruct.

D MICROPHONE CHART

This is a list of a few representative microphones used in typical stage applications. It is meant to provide performance guidelines for specifying a microphone of a particular type. A variety of dynamic, condenser and other microphones should be tried before purchasing any brand.

AKG C 535 EB
Specifications:
Transducer principle: condenser requires 9-52 V phantom power
Polar pattern: cardioid
Frequency range: 20–20,000 Hz
Electrical impedance at 1,000 Hz: 200 ohms
Dimensions: max. diameter=1.9"
Included accessories: stand adapter

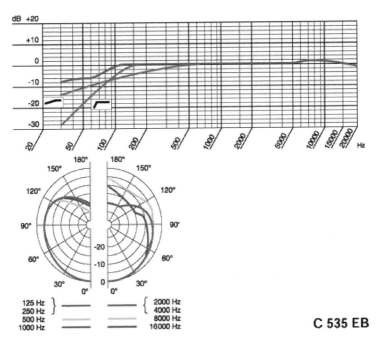

C 535 EB

Shure SM 58
Specifications:
Transducer principle: dynamic (moving coil)
Polar pattern: unidirectional (cardioid), rotationally symmetrical about microphone axis, uniform with frequency
Frequency range: 50 to 15,000 Hz
Nominal impedance: 150 ohms
Dimensions: length=6.4", max. diameter=2"
Included accessories: cable, stand adapter

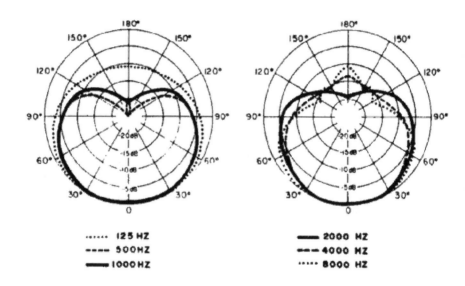

Electro-voice N/D 468
Specifications:
Transducer principle: dynamic
Polar pattern: supercardioid
Frequency range: 80–15,000 Hz
Nominal impedance: 150 ohms
Dimensions: length=6.6", diameter=1.4"
Included accessories: stand adapter

Sony ECM 44B

Specifications:
Transducer principle: electret condenser microphone
Polar pattern: omnidirectional
Frequency range: 40–15,000 Hz
Nominal impedance: 150 ohms
Included accessories: holder clip, urethane windscreen

Sennheiser MKE-2

Specifications:
Transducer principle: electret condenser microphone
Polar pattern: omnidirectional
Dual-diaphragm design virtually eliminates "sweat-outs"
Stranded, stainless-steel reinforced cable provides maximum strength and low
    contact noise
Acoustical equalization via supplied end caps
Successor to the "Broadway-proven" MKE 2 Red Dot

Crown PCC-160

Specifications:
Transducer principle: phase–coherent electret condenser
Polar pattern: half supercardioid
Frequency response: 40–18,000 Hz at 30 degrees incidence
Impedance: 150 ohms
Dimensions: length=6.7", width=3.2"

Neumann KM 184

Specifications:
Type: miniature condenser microphone
Transducer principle: pressure gradient electret condenser
Polar pattern: cardioid
Frequency range: 20 - 20,000 Hz

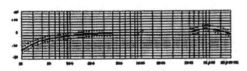
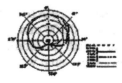

Impedance: 50 ohms
Dimensions: length=107mm, diameter= 22mm

Neumann KMR 821
Specifications:
Type: shotgun
Transducer principle: interference transducer
Impedance: 150 ohms
Frequency range: 20–20,000 Hz
Dimensions: length=226mm, diameter 21mm

C-Ducer
Specifications:
Transducer principle: piezoelectric vibration
Tape length available: 60,200 mm
Frequency response (with pre-amp): 3 dB at 25 Hz and 50 kHz
Included accessories: pre-amp with 1/4" jack output at 5 k ohms

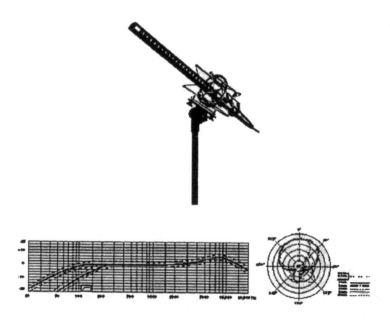

PRODUCT DIRECTORY

Microphones & Accessories

AKG Acoustics
http://www.akg-acoustics.com/

Audio-Technica
http://www.audio-technica.co.uk

Beyerdynamic (GB) Ltd
http://beyerdynamic.co.uk

Crown International, Inc
http://www.crownaudio.com/

Electro-voice
http://www.electrovoice.com/

EVI Audio
http://www.eviaudio.com/

Nady Wireless
http://www.nadywireless.com/

Neumann
http://www.neumannusa.com/

Sennheiser
http://www.sennheiser.com/

Sennheiser USA
http://www.sennheiserusa.com/

Shure Brothers
http://www.shure.com/

Sony
http://www.sel.sony.com/

Telex Communications
http://www.telex.com/

Trantec Systems
http://www.trantec.co.uk

Vega Wireless
http://www.vegawireless.com/

Amplifiers and Processors

Alesis
http://www.alesis.com/

Apogee Sound
http://www.apogee-sound.com/

Aphex Systems
http://www.aphexsys.com/

ART- Applied Research Technology
http://www.artroch.com/

ARX Systems
http://www.arx.com.au

BBE Sound
http://www.bbesound.com/

BGW Systems
http://www.bgw.com/

Bogen Communications
http://www.bogen.com/

Bose
http://www.bose.com/

Crown International, Inc
http://www.crownaudio.com/

EAW
http://www.eaw.com/

Electro-Voice
http://www.electrovoice.com/

EVI Audio
http://www.eviaudio.com/

Peavey
http://www.peavey.com/

QSC Audio
http://www.qscaudio.com/

Rane Corporation
http://www.rane.com/

Soundtech
http://www.soundtech.com/

Yamaha
http://www.yamaha.com/

Loudpeakers

Altec Lansing
http://www.altecmm.com/

Apogee Sound
http://www.apogee-sound.com/

Bose
http://www.bose.com/

Celestion
http://www.celestion.com

Community Loudspeakers
http://www.community.chester.pa.us/

DAS Audio
http://www.dasaudio.com

EAW
http://www.eaw.com/

Electro-Voice
http://www.electrovoice.com/

EVI Audio
http://www.eviaudio.com/

HK Audio
http://www.hkaudio.de

JBL Sound
http://www.jbl.com/

JBL Pro
http://www.jblpro.com/

Klipsch, Inc
http://www.klipsch.com/

Klipsch Pro
http://www.klipschpro.com/

L-Acoustics
http://www.l-acoustics.com

Martin Audio
http://www.martin-audio.com

Meyer Sound
http://www.meyersound.com/

Peavey
http://www.peavey.com/

Renkus - Heinz
http://www.renkus-heinz.com

Soundtech
http://www.soundtech.com/

Tannoy
http://www.tannoy.com

Turbosound
http://www.turbosound.com/

Yamaha
http://www.yamaha.com/

Mixing Consoles

Amek Systems and Controls
http://www.amek.com/

Allen & Heath
http://www.allen-heath.com/

Biamp Systems
http://www.biamp.com/

CADAC
http://www.cada-sound.com

Electro-Voice
http://www.electrovoice.com/

Edcor Electronics
http://www.edcorusa.com/

Euphonix Mixing Systems
http://www.euphonix.com/

EVI Audio
http://www.eviaudio.com/

Formula Sound
http://www.formula-sound.co.uk

Intelix Mixers
http://www.intelix.com/

Klark Teknik
http://www.klarkteknik.com

Lineartech
http://www.lineartechaudio.com/

Level Control Systems
http://www.lcsaudio.com/

Mackie Designs
http://www.mackie.com/

Peavey
http://www.peavey.com/

Soundcraft
http://www.soundcraft.com/

Spirit by SoundCraft (UK)
http://www.soundcraft.com/

Spirit by SoundCraft (USA)
http://www.spiritbysoundcraft.com/

Soundtech
http://www.soundtech.com/

Tascam
http://www.tascam.com/

Yamaha
http://www.yamaha.com/

Signal Processing, Sound Design, Editing & Show Control

ART Products
http://www.artroch.com/

BSS Audio
http://www.bss.co.uk

Clear-com
http://www.clearcom.com/

Cloud Electronics
http://www.cloud.co.uk

Connectronics (Connectors)
http://www.connectronics.co.uk/

dbx Professional
http://www.dbxpro.com/

Denon
http://www.denon.com/

DigiDesign
http://www.digidesign.com/

Dolby
http://www.dolby.com/

Frontier Design Group
http://www.frontierdesign.com/

GLI Pro
http://www.glipro.com/

Lineartech
http://www.lineartechaudio.com/

MIDIman
http://www.midiman.net/

Monster Cable
http://www.monstercable.com/net/

Neutrik (Plugs, Jacks and Patch panels)
http://www.neutrik.com/

Otari Electronics
http://www.otari.com/

Outboard Electronics
http://www.outboard.co.uk/

Richmond Sound Design & Show Control
http://www.show-control.com/

SIA Software Company
http://www.siasoft.com/

Sony
http://www.sel.sony.com/

Stage Research SFX Pro Audio Sound Control
http://www.stageresearch.com/

Tascam
http://www.tascam.com/

Terratec
http://www.terratec-us.com/

Whirlwind (Speaker Cables and Testers)
http://www.whirlwindusa.com/

XTA Electronics
http://www.xta.co.uk

Audio Software

Sonic Foundry Digital Media Tools
http://www.sonicfoundry.com/default.asp

Stardraw Design Tools and Symbol Library
http://www.stardraw.com/

Sound Web Resources
http://www.connectedcourseware.com/ccweb/SoundWeb/Pages/
homepage.htm

Stage Research SFX Pro Audio Sound Control
http://www.stageresearch.com/

Shareware Resources at Carnegie Mellon
http://www.andrew.cmu.edu/~jpino/shareware/sharehome.html

F MUSIC CHRONOLOGY

This chronology is meant to be a guide for those seeking a rudimentary under-standing of musical history. Often a production will require a certain period or musical style. Sound Design has only recently been considered a separate design element. In the early part of the twentieth century, Sound Design was accomplished by the Props Master. A review of the opening for the Chicago Little Theatre in October, 1913 concludes:

Beyond a low, dim hedge looms a rude, red Sunset. Silhouetted against this raw but beautiful Sunset a piping Pan takes a long, melodious Pull at his Pipe. The sound, while remote, is that of a Flute accompanied by a Full Orchestra. Perhaps the Property Man did not know of the orchestra and its fullness when he ordered the Record.

Ancient Greece and Rome
5th century B.C.E. Aulos (flute) and cithara (stringed instrument) depicted in vase paintings

The Middle Ages
590   Church music, Gregorian chants
1000 Troubadours, secular songs in vernacular
1291 Philippe de Vitry, French *Ars Nova*
1300s Percussion and string instruments in Japanese Noh drama
1346 Guillaume de Machaut, French *Ars Nova*
1364 Francesco Landino, organist and composer

The Renaissance
1420 Guillaume Dufay, *Mass in Three Parts*
1500 Diversification of instruments: clavichord, virginal, spinet, harpsichord, violin and lute
1550 *Book of Common Prayer*, Protestant hymn book
1588 English composer William Byrd publishes madrigals
1597 *Sacrae Symphoniae*, religious music by Gabrieli

17th Century

1607 Monteverdi's opera *Orfeo*; first "modern" orchestra with more than 36 instruments

1600s Samisen (stringed instrument) used in Kabuki drama

1674 Giovanni Battista Lully, founder of French opera, directs *Alceste*

1690 Invention of the clarinet

18th Century

1710 Bartolomeo Cristofori develops modern pianoforte in which hammers strike the strings

1712 Antonio Vivaldi composes the twelve concertos known as *Estro Armonico*

1713 Handel writes *Te Deum* and *Jubilate* to celebrate the Peace of Utrecht

1714 Corelli composes *Concerti Grossi*

1721 Bach composes the six *Brandenburg Concertos*

1727 John Gay's *The Beggar's Opera*

1729 Bach's *The Passion According to Saint Matthew* is performed on Good Friday

1740 First public performance of the English anthem *God Save the King*

1741 Handel completes *The Messiah*

1786 Mozart composes *The Marriage of Figaro*, subsequently completes *Don Giovanni, Così fan tutte, The Magic Flute*, the *E Flat, G Minor* and *C*, also known as *The Jupiter Symphony*

1792 French national anthem, *Le Marseillaise*

19th Century

1804 Beethoven composes *Eroica* symphony

1808 Beethoven's *Fifth Symphony*

1822 Schubert's *Symphony No. 8 in B Minor*, called the *Unfinished Symphony*

1824 Beethoven's *Ninth Symphony*

1826 Mendelssohn, *A Midsummer Night's Dream* Overture

1830 Hector Berlioz, *Symphonie fantastique*

1831 Chopin settles in Paris

1840 Robert Schumann writes *Dichterliebe*, songs to poetry by Heine

1844 Berloiz publishes *Treatise on Modern Instrumentation and Orchestration*, which becomes standard work on symphony

orchestras
1848   Stephen Foster writes American folk-music *Oh! Susanna*
1853   Franz Liszt composes *Sonata in B Minor*, finest composition for the piano in the romantic era
1867   Johann Strauss, the younger, *The Blue Danube Waltz* Moussorgsky's *Night on the Bare Mountain*
1874   Strauss, *Die Fledermaus*
1876   Richard Wagner, *Der Ring des Nibelungen,* Tchaikovsky composes music for *Swan Lake* Edvard Grieg writes *Peer Gynt Suites* Brahms scores *C Minor* (1876), *D Major* (1877) *F Major* (1883) and *E Minor* (1885)
1878   Gilbert and Sullivan, *H.M.S. Pinafore*
1884   Rimsky-Korsakov composes *Scheherazade*
1889   César Franck, *Symphony in D Minor*
1893   Antonin Dvorák, *Fifth Symphony From the New World*
1894   Claude Debussy, impressionist school of music, *L'Après midi d'une Faune*
1896   Strauss, *Also Sprach Zarathustra*

20th Century
1900   Sibelius' *Finlandia*
1902   Gustav Mahler, *Third Symphony*
1910   Gabriel Fauré's piano composition *Nine Preludes* Igor Stravinsky, *Firebird*
1912   Maurice Ravel's *Daphne et Chloé Suite*
1919   Manuel de Falla's *The Three-Cornered-Hat* ballet
1924   George Gershwin's *Rhapsody in Blue* Arthur Schoenberg, *Suite for Piano* Respighi's *Pines of Rome*
1925   Duke Ellington organizes his first band Aaron Copland's *Symphony for Organ and Orchestra*
1928   Ravel's *Bolero*
1935   Gershwin's *Porgy and Bess*
1936   Sergei Prokofiev's music for *Peter and the Wolf*
1937   Dimitri Shostakovich, *Fifth Symphony* Béla Bartók's *Music for String Instruments, Percussion and Celestra*
1939   Charles Ives' *Second Piano Sonata* performed (written between 1904 and 1915)

1943   Rodgers and Hammerstein's *Oklahoma!*

1944   Aaron Copland's *Appalachian Spring*

1956   Karlheinz Stockhausen creates an electronic music composition, *Gesang der Junglinge*

1958   Pierre Boulez writes *Improvisation sur Mellarme*

1962   United States tour of the Beatles

1969   Woodstock, *HPSCHD*

1972   Leonard Bernstein's *Mass* opens JFK Center

1977   Robert Wilson, *Einstein on the Beach*

1987   Rock Group Chicago's "MIDI" Tour

1990s   Digitally "sampled" music in concerts & CDs

2000   MP3 and Napster "rip" CDs for sharing; lawsuit by music industry

G CUE SHEETS

The cue sheet should be organized in such a way that it is clear and easy to read. The section below from *Two Can Play* by Trevor Rhone is used as an example to illustrate where the cues occur in the script. Bold parentheses next to cues added for clarity, italicized parentheses are in the script. Note: This is an example of a script with sound cues indicated. The cue sheet follows along with a blank cue sheet template that you may copy for your own use.

Cue #	Act/Scene	Description of Effect	Source	Start Cue	Time		Output level @	Notes
					Duration	Fade Time		
						In	Out		
1	Act 1 Sc 1	Reggae music	CD	pre-show	5 min	0	6 sec	-10db	fade out in blackout
2	"	gunshots, dogs	MD	in BO	12 sec	0	3 sec	-5db	follow #1 fade in BO
3	"	single shot, barking	MD	"Yes, Jim"	8 sec	0	0	-5db	quick cue
4	"	closer gunshots	MD	"is wa"	5 sec	0	0	-5db	quick cue
5	"	barrage of loud shots	MD	"yuh head"	5 sec	0	0	-5db	quick cue
6	"	footsteps	MD	"listen"	12 sec	0	0	-5db	radio version only
7	"	water faucet	MD	offstage	8 sec	0	0	-5db	glass fills with water

Cue #	Act/Scene	Description of Effect	Source	Start Cue	Time				Output level @	Notes
					Duration	Fade Time				
						In	Out			

H REFERENCE BOOKS

Audio Engineer's Reference Book
Michael Talbot-Smith (Editor) / Paperback / Published 1998, Focal Press

Audio Systems Technology #2 - Handbook For Installers And Engineers
Ray Alden, NSCA / Paperback / Published 1998, Butterworth-Heinemann

The Complete Handbook of Public Address Sound Systems
Frederick Alton Everest / Published 1978, Tab Books

Handbook for Sound Engineers : The New Audio Encyclopedia
Glen M. Ballou (Editor) / Hardcover / Published 1991, Focal Press

The Home Studio Guide to Microphones
Loren Alldrin, et al / Paperback / Published 1998, Hal Leonard Publishing
Corporation

**Life on the Road : The Incredible Rock and Roll Adventures of Dinky
Dawson**
Dinky Dawson, Carter Alan / Paperback / Published 1998, Watson-Guptill
Publications

The Master Handbook of Acoustics
F. Alton Everest / Paperback / Published 1994, McGraw-Hill Education

Modern Audio Technology : A Handbook for Technicians and Engineers
Martin Clifford / Reissued 1993, Prentice Hall PTR

**Mr. Bernds Goes to Hollywood : My Early Life and Career in Sound
Recording at Columbia With Frank Capra and Others (Scarecrow
Filmmakers Series, No 65)**
Edward Bernds / Hardcover / Published 1999, Scarecrow Press

Newnes Audio & Hi-Fi Engineer's Pocket Book
Vivian Capel / Hardcover / Published 1994, Focal Press

Practical Recording Techniques
Bruce Bartlett, Jenny Bartlett / Published 2002, Focal Press

Professional Microphone Techniques
David Mills Huber, et al / Paperback / Published 1999

**Proceedings of the ASME Noise Control and Acoustics Division :
Presented at the 1996 ASME International Mechanical Engineering
Congress and exposition** T. M. Farabee(Editor), American Society of
Mechanical Engineers Hardcover / Published 1996

Light and Sound for Engineers
Reginald Cyril Stanley / Published 1968, Nelson

Sound and Music for Theatre
Kaye & Lebrecht / Published 1999, Focal Press

Stereo Microphone Techniques
Bruce Bartlett / Paperback / Published 1991, Focal Press

Television and Audio Handbook : For Technicians and Engineers
K. Blair Benson, Jerry C. Whitaker / Published 1990 McGraw-Hill Education

**Tonmeister Technology : Recording Environments, Sound Sources, and
Microphone Techniques**
Michael Dickretter / Paperback / Published 1989, Temmer Enterprises

Sound Studio Construction on a Budget
F. Alton Everest / Paperback / Published 1996, McGraw-Hill Companies

Sound Engineer's Pocket Book
Michael Talbot-Smith (Editor) / Hardcover / Published 1995, Focal Press

I PROFESSIONAL ORGANISATIONS

Audio Engineering Society (AES)
http://www.aes.org/

Advanced Television Systems Committee (ATSC)
http://www.atsc.org/

Music Producers Guild of the Americas (MPGA)
http://www.musicproducer.org/

National Association of Broadcasters (NAB)
http://www.nab.org/

The National Academy of Recording Arts & Sciences, Inc (NARAS)
http://grammy.aol.com/

Society of Motion Pictures and Television Engineers (SMPTE)
http://www.smpte.org/

The United States Institute for Theatre Technology (USITT)
http://www.usitt.org/

J GLOSSARY OF TERMS

acoustic suspension - a type of loudspeaker which uses a closed-box.

acoustic coupling - connecting loudspeaker drivers together to achieve greater gain. The principle is also used in the Bose 901 loudspeaker with identical drivers hooked in series. Since "coupled" this way they cannot all resonate at the same frequency, the drivers divide into the different frequencies to reproduce sound.

AES/EBU - (Audio Engineering Society / European Broadcast Union) is a digital audio standard. Most consumer and professional digital audio devices (CD players, DAT decks, etc.) that feature digital audio I/O support AES/EBU. AES/EBU is a bit-serial communications protocol for transmitting digital audio data through a single transmission line.

AFL - an acronym for "after fade listen," which describes a means of monitoring the signal post fader solo.

alnico magnet - a magnet made from aluminum and nickel alloy used in loudspeaker drivers.

amplifier - a device which enables an input signal to control power from a source independent of the signal and thus be capable of delivering an output which bears some relationship to, and is generally greater than, the input signal.

anechoic chamber - a room in which reflected sound is practically eliminated. Used for measuring the characteristics of loudspeakers and microphones.

assign - used in mixers to designate the routing or switching of a signal to a particular path, such as a group output or auxiliary.

attack - how fast gain changes after threshold has been exceeded.

attenuate - to lower the volume of a signal.

attenuator (loss pad) - an electronic device inserted between microphone and preamplifier which, through resistance, eliminates input overload by lowering microphone output.

audiophile - an individual who seeks perfection in the recording and reproduction of sound. The discriminating listener can be considered in this category, but the fanatic is known to spend large sums of money in pursuit of the ideal.

auxiliary - an additional output path assignment in a mixer which allows the connection of external devices either pre- or post- fader, or to set up several independent mixes for different musicians. These can be grouped via a bus network, or used individually for each input module, depending on the design of the mixing console.

azimuth adjustment - the adjustment to position the head gap exactly perpendicular to the horizontal base of the tape.

baffle - the panel to which most speakers are mounted, usually the front panel of an enclosure.

balanced input - interconnectors utilize two conductors plus a ground, usually to the cable shield. Three pins are necessary with balanced inputs. Also known as low level, 600 ohm, Lo-Z or microphone input. However, this type of connection is used for more than just microphones.

bandwidth - the audio frequency range. In digitally sampled sound, bandwidth is determined by sampling rate.

bass reflex - a type of speaker enclosure that has an opening which permits rear sound waves to emerge in phase with sound from the front.

beam splitter - a partial mirror that allows a laser beam to pass through in one direction and be reflected back to an optical sensor.

bias - a high frequency alternating current fed into the recording circuit and used as a carrier of the audio signals to the record head, as well as current to the erase head.

bits per sample - numbers are stored in digital memories as groups of binary digits, called bits. Each bit in a sample accounts for a factor of two in the accuracy of a digital number. Thus, if a sample is recorded as an eight-bit number, that means the dynamic range of the input waveform is divided into 256 (two raised to the eighth power) possible levels, and one of those levels is what is recorded.

boost - increasing the signal level. Often refers to raising the level of bass or treble frequencies during equalization.

bridging - the shunting of one signal circuit by one or more circuits usually for the purpose of deriving one or more circuit branches.

bulk eraser - a strong alternating electro-magnetic device used to erase the magnetic patterns on tape while still wound on a reel, or in bulk form.

bus - a common electrical connection for multiple circuits. In a mixer, a bus

carries signals from a number of inputs to an output or auxiliary channel fader.
boundary - any large acoustically hard surface such as a floor, wall, ceiling where the microphone assembly is placed.

capstan - the rotating shaft which engages the tape and pulls it across the heads at constant speed.
cardioid - microphone with a heart-shaped polar response, making it most sensitive in one direction.
channel - an input or output path in an audio circuit.
chorusing - an effect involving delays, pitch change and panning.
clipping - severe distortion which is the result of excessive gain. The waves are "clipped" below their peak as the signal exceeds the capacity of the amplifier circuit.
compressor - a transducer which, for a given input amplitude range, produces a smaller output range. Also a variable gain amplifier which has a fixed gain that doesn't affect output level until the input level exceeds a given dynamic threshold.
condenser microphone - a microphone which has a diaphragm consisting of a movable plate of a condenser (capacitor). When polarized by applying a direct current voltage, motion of the diaphragm in relation to a fixed backplate produces an output voltage.
cone - diaphragm of a conventional moving coil loudspeaker.
CPS - cycles per second.
cross talk - signal leakage between two channels.
crossover network - in multiple loudspeaker systems, a circuit employing electrical filters of frequency discriminating paths for routing high, low and middle frequencies to the particular speakers designed to handle them.
cut - decreasing the signal level. Often used to describe reducing bass or treble levels during equalization.

damping (of a loudspeaker) - expresses the ability of the cone to stop moving as soon as the electrical input signal ceases. Poor damping allows motion to continue briefly like an automobile with poor shock absorbers. This hangover creates a 'booming' sound in the bass frequencies masking clarity.
damping factor - ratio of loudspeaker impedance to amplifier source impedance. A large ratio improves loudspeaker damping.
DAT - digital audio tape. Recording tape that uses sampling and digital data to

store sound. Also refers to the player.

dB (decibel) - a relative measure of sound intensity. One dB is the smallest change in sound volume that the human ear can detect. Also used to express logarithmically voltage and power ratios.

degaussing - the process of de-magnetizing tape recorder heads and metal parts of the tape transport mechanism.

delay - an effect commonly used in contemporary recordings which produces independently variable left and right channel signal delays. The result is a "doubled" sound.

demagnetizer - a device for removing magnetic force fields from tape heads and metal parts of the tape transport mechanism.

detent - a "click-stop" point in the travel of a knob or slider.

diaphragm - sound generating element of a loudspeaker.

directional characteristics - ability to respond to different sound waves in relation to their incoming location.

distortion - any difference between the original sound and the recorded and reproduced sound.

distortion, harmonic - nonlinear distortion of a system or transducer characterized by the appearance in the output of harmonics other than the fundamental component when the input wave is sinusoidal.

distortion, intermodulation - nonlinear distortion of a system or transducer characterized by the appearance in the output of frequencies equal to the sums and differences of integral multiples of the two or more component frequencies present in the input wave.

Doppler effect - the change in pitch of a sound heard by an observer when the sound source is in motion. It is called the Doppler effect after an Austrian, Christian Johann Doppler (1803-53), who first explained it.

dry - lacking reverberation, as in a "dry" auditorium, or without EQ or special effect (e.g. dry and wet sources)

dubbing - the act of duplicating on tape.

dynamic microphone - an electro-magnetic type which employs a moving coil in a magnetic field.

dynamic range - the ratio between the overload level and the minimum acceptable signal level in a system or transducer.

echo - a wave which has been reflected or otherwise returned with sufficient magnitude and delay to be perceived in some manner as a wave distinct from that directly transmitted.

editing - selection of certain sections of tape recordings and the deletion of unwanted portions and then splicing them together in the desired sequence.

effects - altering the sound signal with electronic or LSI (large scale integration) technology to create natural reverberation, echo, delay, flanging, pitch changes or other effects.

electronic crossover - a method of dividing frequencies sent to loudspeakers using an electronic circuit.

equalization - the manipulation of frequencies that are required to meet the recognized standards of recording and reproducing techniques.

EQ curve - a graph of the equalization response with frequency on the horizontal axis and amplitude on the vertical axis.

erase head - the magnetic assembly on tape recorder over which the tape passes to remove previously recorded signals.

fader - a potentiometer that controls the loudness of a signal.

feed reel - the reel on a tape recorder which supplies the tape.

feedback - a howl produced in a sound system that occurs when the output of the loudspeaker enters the microphone or guitar pickup and is re-amplified.

filter - a simple equalizer designed to eliminate ranges of frequencies, such as a high pass filter which cuts the lows, allowing the highs to pass.

flange effect - combination of delay and low frequency oscillation modulation. It can dramatically thicken the sound of keyboard or produce the aircraft sound popular among guitarists. The resultant variations in pitch and stereo imaging are known as "flanging."

flat response - any audio system is specified as having an essentially flat frequency response if it is rated plus or minus 3 dB from 50 to 15,000 Hz.

Fletcher-Munson curve - a sensitivity curve plotted for the human ear showing its characteristic for different intensity levels between the threshold of hearing and the threshold of feeling. These data are often referred to as equal loudness contours.

flutter - very short and rapid variations in tape speed.

frequency - the rate of repetition in cycles per second of musical pitch, as well as of electrical signals. Low frequencies refer to bass tone, high frequencies to treble tone.

frequency response - the manner in which the output of a device responds to and varies with changes in input frequency. A "flat response" microphone, for example, indicates near-equal response over the entire range of frequencies. In obtaining optimum performance, frequency response is often "tailored" by introducing low-frequency "rolloff" and controlled high-frequency "boost." These rolloffs and boosts must be accomplished smoothly and abrupt variations in the frequency response curve indicate poor microphone quality.

frequency spectrum analysis - using a real-time analyzer to see the various frequencies that are present in a particular sound.

gain - the increase in signal provided by an amplifier between input level and output level.

graphic equalizer - a particular type of equalizer which operates simultaneously on a relatively large number of frequency bands. May adjust 27 bands 1/3 octave wide or 11 bands almost an octave wide. Each band has its own slider control for boost and cut, and these controls are arranged on the front panel in order of increasing frequency horizontally left to right, and increasing gain vertically, thereby giving a graphic representation of the chosen frequency response.

ground - a point in any electrical system that has zero voltage, usually the chassis of any electrical component.

Haas effect - a psychoacoustic effect in which the time of arrival of a sound to the left and right ears affects our perception of direction. The first sound to be heard takes command of the ear, and sound arriving up to 50 milliseconds later seems to arrive as a part of and from the same directions as the original sound.

head - an electro-magnetic device across which the tape is drawn and which magnetizes the oxide coating of tape (or other types like chromium dioxide).

head alignment - in tape recorders, the correct position of the tape head and gap, with respect to the magnetic tape.

Hz (Hertz)- a unit measuring frequency and equals one cycle per second.

horns - compression drivers mounted in metal, fiberglass or plastic enclosures for high frequency reproduction.

hum - low frequency noise in an audio component usually induced from the power line or stray magnetic or electrostatic fields.

impedance - a common characteristic of electrical devices expressed in ohms. It is the AC resistance of any electrical system, a measure of the extent to which a substance opposes movement of electrons. Audio equipment is generally referred to as either "high" or "low" impedance. Microphones are classified as either high Z (10,000 ohms and up) or low Z (50 ohms to 250 ohms). Low-Z microphones permit the use of longer cables without high-frequency rolloff. For best results in connecting two components, output and input impedances must match.

information surface - the surface of a laser disc, usually aluminum or tellurium, on which pits are read using a laser diode to code sound signals as digital data. A high power laser is used to burn the pits into a master glass surface in the manufacturing process.

input - the receptacle or jack through which a signal is fed into an amplifier.

IPS - abbreviation for tape speed in inches per second.

jack - receptacle or plug connector leading to the input or output circuit of a tape recorder or other component.

knee - a sharp bend in a response curve of an EQ or signal processor.

laser diode - a solid state laser used in compact disc players to detect pits and reflective surfaces.

lavalier microphone - a microphone designed to be worn around the neck or attached by a clip to the clothing.

LED - light emitting diode. Used as an indicator light.

level indicator - indicates the level at which the recording is being made and serves as a warning against under recording or over recording. It may be in the form of LED indicators or a VU meter.

line level - also known as unbalanced level. Inputs are high impedance, usually around 10 k ohms.

mains - refers to main electric power feed for equipment, or to the primary loudspeakers used for output from a mixer via amplifiers.

microphone - a transducer which converts sound into an electrical output or voltage.

micron - one millionth of a meter. Pits in the information surface of a compact disc are 0.1 microns deep.

MIDI - musical instrument digital interface. A standard to connect electronic instruments to controllers and each other.

mil - 1/1000 of an inch. Tape thickness is usually measured in mils.

mixer - a device by which signals from two or more sources can be combined and fed simultaneously into a tape recorder at the proper level and balance.

monaural - signal limited to a single channel.

monitor - checking signals during a recording or playback by listening on a separate loudspeaker or by watching a level meter.

NAB curve - standard playback equalization curve set by the National Association of Broadcasters.

noise - undesired sound such as crosstalk, hum, hiss.

Nyquist frequency - refers to the highest frequency a given device can safely sample.

Ohm's law - an equation which expresses the relationship between voltage (E), amperage (I) and resistance (R). It is E=IR.

optical sensor - a device within a compact disc player that reads the reflected pattern of light.

oscillator - a device for producing a continuous electrical oscillation, or pure tone, at any desired frequency. Often oscillators are built into mixers or tape decks to provide a constant signal for checking the throughput (continuity path).

oscilloscope - a device which forms a graphic representation of an electrical signal on a screen (cathode ray tube). Used for testing and measuring of electrical and electronic equipment.

output - the signal voltage coming from components, such as pre-amplifiers and amplifiers. In tape recorders, there are line outputs, speaker outputs and monitor outputs.

oxide - as used in magnetic tape - a microscopic ferrous oxide.

overload distortion - distortion caused by too great an input signal to an amplifier or preamplifier. This distortion is not controlled by volume control setting and most frequently occurs when microphones are used close to the sound source. It is controllable with an attenuator.

pad - a nonadjustable passive network which reduces the power level of a signal without introducing appreciable distortion.

pan pot - places a signal across two stereo lines (left and right). Turning it to the left will send all of the signal to the left line, and to the right, all of the signal will be sent to the right side. If the pan pot is placed at the center position, an equal amount of signal will be fed to both sides and the image in the stereo picture will be central.

parametric equalization - an equalizer with the most flexibility, since there are many parameters that can be adjusted, such as varying frequency, amount of boost and cut, and the bandwidth of the activity.

passive crossover - consits of large coils of wire and huge capacitors inserted between the output of the power amp and speaker. They are designed to cut out the treble to the bass speaker and cut out the bass tones to the treble driver.

patch cord - a short cable with a plug at either end used to interconnect equipment, such as tape recorders and amplifiers.

PFL - pre fade listen. This button will solo the signal on the monitors, and the feed for this solo is taken before the fader.

phantom power - a method of supplying necessary voltage to a condenser or electret microphone without the use of batteries. Typical voltages are between +18VDC and +48VDC. ONLY used with a balanced line. Feeds a D.C. voltage down the same line. Blocking capacitors keep the D.C. voltage from straying into the audio sections of the mixer.

phase cancellation - occurs when two similar or identical signals are out of step in time. Waveforms displaced by 180 degrees tend to cancel.

phasing - the polarity orientation of the two speakers used in stereo playback. Also refers to polarity orientation of microphone connectors and a delay effect.

phone jack - female ¼" connector. Used with male phone plug.

pinch roller - a rubber roller which engages the capstan and pulls the tape with constant speed and prevents slippage.

piston range - the efective excursion range of a driver. Determines the lowest frequencies a driver can produce.

pitch change - to change the tone of an input signal. Digital effects processors can change pitch in semitone increments over a plus/minus one-octave range. Fine adjustment of pitch in one-cent (1/100th of a semitone) increments/decrements is also possible.

playback head - the magnetic head which picks up signals from tape for playback.

plug - a form of mechanical interconnector used for quick and easy connection of components, such as phone plug, phono plug and AC plug.

polar pattern - response graph of microphone sensitivity through a 360 degree axis.

pop filter - an acoustically transparent shield placed above the microphone diaphragm, often placed around the exterior of the microphone, which sharply reduces the bad effects of explosive vocal sounds but does not affect desired microphone performance.

pop sensitivity - the measure of a microphone's reaction to explosive vocal sounds, like "P," "T," and "F." A microphone with high pop sensitivity will create a very disturbing low-frequency "boom" in the sound system. Microphone types vary widely in their pop sensitivity.

post-fader - describes an auxiliary send affected by the setting of the channel fader.

potentiometer - a variable resistor used for volume and tone controls.

power amplifier - an amplifier designed to operate a speaker system.

power cord - cable used to connect a component to AC current.

pre-amplifier - an amplifier that boosts extremely weak signal voltages, such as those from microphones, magnetic playback heads or phonograph pickups, to a level that is usable by power amplifiers, and at the same time accomplishes the necessary equalization for industry standards.

pre-fader - describes an auxiliary send unaffected by the setting of the channel fader.

print through - when tapes are stored for long periods of time in a tightly wrapped configuration the magnetism can be exchanged, thus signals recorded can transfer to adjacent pieces of tape, resulting in mixed sounds when the tape is played back.

proximity effect - emphasis on bass response in microphones. Singers take advantage of this when they get close to the mic.

psychoacoustics - the interaction of human perception and architectural/mechanical characteristics of environment.

RCA jack - inexpensive connector used in consumer audio gear.

release - how fast gain returns to unity after input signal foes below threshold.

resonant frequency - the tendency of any physical body to vibrate most freely at one particular frequency as a result of excitation by a sound of that particular frequency.

return - line input for signals after signal processing.

reverberation - the persistence of sound within a space after the source of that sound has ceased.

RIAA equalization - in vinyl recording an equalizer is used to reduce the lows and boost the highs when all master recordings are cut, otherwise, the stylus that cuts the master would vibrate out of its groove if a full deep bass tone was fed to it. The RIAA (Recording Institute Association of America) curve becomes audible only if it is uncorrected by the manufacturer of your pre-amp, amplifier and speakers.

SCMS - (Serial Copy Management System) used by MD decks to allow only first generation digital copies to be made of premastered software via the deck's digital input jack. Usually unlimited analog copies may be made, but this limitation affects your ability to make digital copies of your original recordings.

S/P-DIF - (Sony/Philips Digital Interface Format) typically refers to AES/ EBU operated in consumer mode over unbalanced RCA cable.

shelving - describes the shape of an EQ response where the response curve flattens out.

signal-to-noise ratio - the ratio, measured in dB's, between the pure sound and the noise induced by the recording system itself.

simul sync - technique of recording sound on sound by mixing a recording from one track with a subsequent recording on another track. During this process, the record head is used as a playback head to synchronize the sound.

slate - routes the control room microphone signal to all the buses in a mixer for announcing on tape the name of the recording or take number. In some consoles, a low-frequency tone is put on the tape during slating so that the beginning of the take can be quickly located by listening for tape tones during fast forward or rewind.

slew rate - the speed at which a transistor tracks a rapidly changing input signal. Slewing rate is expressed in volts-per-microsecond. A slew rate of 32 volts/microsecond means that a transistor is capable of passing a voltage change from 1 to 32 volts in one-millionth of a second.

SPL (sound pressure level) - volume, loudness of sound, expressed as a logarithmic ratio of intensity. 0 dB SPL reference is approximately the threshold of human hearing at 1000 Hz.

spider - a circular piece of spring-like corrugated fabric used to guide the movement of the voice coil so that it remains centered in the narrow slot of the magnetic assembly.

splicing - joining together of two pieces of tape while editing.

splicing block - a device for holding the two pieces of tape to be spliced while they are being attached.

splicing tape - a special pressure sensitive non-magnetic tape used for splicing magnetic tape.

sweep EQ - an equalizer that allows you to continuously vary the frequency.

take-up reel - the reel located on the right side of the tape recorder which accumulates the tape as it is recorded or played.

tape guides - grooved metal posts located on either side of the head assembly to keep the tape tracking properly across the heads.

tape index counter - a digital counter used mostly to aid in referring to a particular portion of tape.

tape speed - the speed at which tape moves past the heads and measured in inches per second.

tape splicer - a semi-automatic or automatic device used for splicing tape.

tape transport - the mechanical portion of the tape recorder mounted with motors, reel spindles, heads and controls. It does not include pre-amplifiers, speakers or carrying case.

tension arm - a part of the tape transport mechanism on a tape recorder that keeps the correct tightness on the tape. It may be used as a switch to detect when the tape is no longer present. At the end of the tape, the recorder will switch off automatically.

timbre - the characteristic quality of a musical instrument which permits it to be distinguished from another. Timbre depends on the harmonic or overtone structure of the instrument.

transducer - device for converting from one form of energy to another, e.g. a microphone converts from acoustic to electrical, a loudspeaker driver converts from electrical to acoustical.

transistor - a semiconductor device, invented by Dr. William Shockley, Dr. John Barden, and Dr. Walter H. Brattain of the Bell Telephone Laboratories in 1948. The name "transistor" is coined from two words, transfer and resistor. The first transistor consisted of a particle of semiconductor material, such as germanium, mounted in a holder with two point contacts.

turntable - a device, soon to be a relic, which spins a vinyl record at a constant speed using a belt- or direct-driven motor. It must also have a tonearm and cartridge to pick-up the sounds out of the record grooves.

tweeter - a driver designed to reproduce only the high frequencies of the audible spectrum.

unbalanced input - interconnections utilize one conductor and the shield is used for the other conductor and ground. Only two pins are necessary with unbalanced inputs. Also known as high level, Hi-Z or line level input.

vented box - a loudspeaker enclosure that has an open port to the outside permitting sound waves to emerge in phase.

voice coil - the metal coil of a dynamic loudspeaker.

VOM - volt ohm meter. Used to test continuity and voltage.

VU meter - a volume unit meter which indicates the relative levels of sounds being recorded.

wet - signal after it has been changed with an effect such as reverb, flanging, pitch change or delay.

woofer - a low frequency cone driver.

working distance - the distance from the performer or instrument to the microphone.

wow - repetitive slow variations in tape speed.

XLR - a three pin connector used for microphones and balanced connections. Also known as a "Cannon" connector after one of the first manufacturers.

INDEX

ENTERTAINMENT TECHNOLOGY PRESS

FREE SUBSCRIPTION SERVICE

Keeping Up To Date with

Sound For The Stage

Entertainment Technology Press titles are continually up-dated, and all changes and additions are listed in date order in the relevant dedicated area of the publisher's website. Simply go to the front page of www.etnow.com and click on the BOOKS button. From there you can locate the title and be connected through to the latest information and services related to the publication, including the tender specification examples in this book available for download.

The author can be contacted by email: finelli@arts.usf.edu